Pure OCD

The Invisible Side of Obsessive-Compulsive Disorder

Chrissie Hodges

Edited by Ethan Raath

ISBN: 978-1-63491-991-3

Published by BookLocker.com, Inc., St. Petersburg, Florida, U.S.A.

Printed on acid-free paper.

BookLocker.com, Inc.
2017

First Edition

This memoir is dedicated to the fearless and dedicated advocates for mental health. In selflessly sharing their stories, they eliminate stigma and foster hope in those who suffer with mental illness.

The publishing of this memoir is dedicated to my partner, Sean David McLimans. It is through his love, compassion, and support that I can truly believe in the power of accomplishing anything I put my mind to.

Table of Contents

Chapter 1: My Living Hell

"God Himself would reject anyone at Heaven's gates who took the liberty to take a life rightfully God's and God's only to take."

My mind drifted, recalling those sentiments in a sermon I heard years ago with the preacher damning any person succeeding in suicide to Hell. The image of him ranting on the selfishness and weak-mindedness tempting anyone to complete such an atrocious act became clear, even in my clouded mind. I faintly heard his words echoing around me. I shivered, not from the cold but from how those words impacted me. The memory burst wide open. I could almost smell the strong oak beams holding up the tiny chapel's ceiling. Worship bulletins acted as fans to the congregation sweltering from the lack of air conditioning in the sanctuary. I pictured myself sweating and panicking in the creaky, wooden pew.

The shame and fear conjured up by the pastor's words hammered me to a miniscule size. His eyes bore into mine, tearing open a bleeding heart, and shattering a soul already falling toward rock bottom at a rapid pace. He stared into me as if he could read my thoughts. *Does he know the secrets I carry?* I had decided long before that day in chapel suicide would be a welcomed option if I could no longer bear the brunt of the madness in my mind. *Maybe he knows?* His angry words shook my brain, sending a surge of fear up my spine. I felt guilty for hating him. The service concluded and I walked out of the small, backwoods chapel wondering if he was really speaking the word of God. I certainly hope not.

Today, lying alone and scared in an ice cold creek bed, I questioned if he may be right about going to Hell? I held my hands over the open wound in my stomach, protecting it from splitting open any farther. It wouldn't matter anymore if it did. I passed the point of pain from the self-inflicted knife wound half an hour ago. My rational mind intervened, confirming whatever Hell may be, it could not be worse than living inside my tormented mind. I would gladly accept a physical Hell for eternity, than live one more day in the hell I had experienced since I was 8 years old.

Chapter 2: The First Obsession

It was a typical Thursday in third grade. Nothing out of the ordinary happened in the weeks leading up to this particular day. I was having a normal day as a social, outgoing, and energetic student cracking jokes with classmates as usual. Sometimes it got me in trouble, but generally I was a good student with good manners.

We filed into the classroom after lunch, settling into our seats. The teacher had us working quietly at our desks before resuming afternoon classes. Our classroom was organized into rows from front to back and side to side with spaces in between each desk. Mine was positioned by the pathway to the door of the classroom. I sat 4 seats back on the left side facing the door. I was focused on a reading assignment when a kid in my class named Jeff bolted past me from the front of the room. This was not out of the ordinary, but today my internal antenna warned me something bad was happening.

A tingling sensation on the back of my neck began radiating into my head. It felt like a heat wave in my neck, traveling down into my chest, arms, and hands. My forearms and hands became numb and my breathing began to quicken. My brain was screaming to run away, but I didn't understand what I would be running from. I looked around feeling like the walls and ceiling were closing in on me.

Don't look back, Chrissie...Stay focused, Chrissie...Keep breathing, Chrissie.

I heard the teacher urgently telling Jeff to run quickly to the bathroom. I closed my eyes tightly, holding my breath. I felt his energy sprinting up the pathway toward the door. My body cringed and everything slowed down as he approached my desk.

Oh God, please make it past me, Oh God, please make it past me.

My prayers were too late. Out of the corner of my eye I saw him bend over and throw up inches from my desk. In one swift motion, my legs powered me as far away from Jeff and his sickness as possible. When I finally opened my eyes, the boy sitting next to me was desperately trying to push me off his lap. I was in a fetal position between him and his desk, feeling unable to breathe. He finally shoved me onto the floor, and I hit the ground with a hard thud.

I was sweating profusely, terrified by what just happened. I looked up to see the majority of attention was not on Jeff and his sickness, but on me. The teacher was in my face shaking me and yelling, but I couldn't hear her words. All I could hear was my heartbeat and labored breathing. As the world came into focus, my teacher was asking if I was okay. All eyes were on me. I was humiliated. I needed to figure out what just happened, but I didn't know if I could talk. I worried if I said what I felt out loud, it may happen again.

I was shaking as my teacher helped me stand up. I heard a few snickers from students and I shot them a threatening look. This wasn't my fault, but I was embarrassed. I wanted to crack a joke or something to make everything look okay, but I was too overwhelmed and shaken up. I couldn't look back at my desk. Every time I thought about what happened, I felt the hot feeling and tingling in my neck again.

Why is this happening to me? What is this weird physical feeling? Am I going to throw up? Does this mean I might throw up? What if this feeling happens again in front of everyone?

I could feel the heat rising in my chest and my hands started to tingle.

OH GOD, HERE IT COMES AGAIN, WHAT DO I DO? HOW DO I GET OUT OF HERE?

I wanted to run as fast as I could out of the classroom. I wanted to run as far as I could away from school, my teacher, and the student who threw up. I hated everyone in this classroom. How could everyone be so calm after what just happened? Why are people acting like nothing happened? Why didn't anyone else care as much as I did? Why do I care so much?

Every year kids get sick in the classroom and I've never reacted or felt this way. My sister will throw up if you look at her the wrong way and it has never bothered me. I've thrown up and while I don't find it exciting, I've never felt this way about it. What happened to make things different today? Was it the student? Was it because it happened so close to me? It doesn't make sense. Why all of a sudden am I feeling this way about throwing up?

I pressed my face against the cool window, staring at the playground. How I wished I was outside in the open air instead of breathing contaminated throw up air. I looked over at my chair and my body began reacting again. I couldn't breathe. I needed to control this feeling right now. I started counting my breaths to distract myself. How many breaths does it take for this bad feeling to go away?

One breath...two breaths...three breaths...four breaths....Okay, the tingling feeling is going away...five breaths...six breaths...Okay, I can breathe normally now.

My teacher put her hand on my back, leading me to the chair in front of her desk. She asked me questions, but I didn't want to tell her what happened. For some reason I felt embarrassed and ashamed. Wouldn't she think I was an idiot? Also, wouldn't saying it out loud prove it really happened? I don't want to believe it was real. It couldn't have been real. Maybe I imagined it? But, whenever I looked toward my desk, the hot feeling started again. I counted breaths to make it stop knowing it only takes six breaths to stop it. I had to stay at six. I had a feeling anything over six would be bad. If I couldn't get things under control by six breaths, there is no telling what could happen?

Just as I began feeling calm and prepared to go back to my desk, Jeff came back into the room. He was walking toward me and the teacher's desk. I started panicking. I didn't want to breathe the same air he was breathing. *Oh God, I cannot be near him. Oh God, what if I throw up? What if I catch whatever he has and I throw up later today or tomorrow? HOW CAN I GET OUT OF HERE? I HAVE TO GET OUT OF HERE!*

"Excuse me, I need to go to the bathroom, please it's an emergency," I told my teacher, already getting out of my chair to avoid the student.

"Okay, Chrissie. Are you okay?" she asked.

I bolted from the classroom without answering. I needed air. I was trapped in there with Jeff and his throw up. Why is this happening? Everything was fine before Jeff got sick. I hate him so much! I will never talk to him again for what he did. He has ruined my life!

I splashed water on my face and looked at myself in the bathroom mirror. My chest and neck were covered in red splotches. I felt scared. Seeing physical evidence meant what happened was real. I wanted to believe it was a fluke. Maybe it's just a bad day? How could everything be different in one second? What did I do to deserve this? I prayed for God to have mercy on me and take these bad feelings away. Maybe God was doing this to me? How could He let something this horrible happen to me? Did I do something wrong to make Him mad at me?

I stayed in the bathroom peeking around the corner at our classroom until I saw Jeff being escorted out with his books. He was going home, so it was safe to go back to the classroom. I returned to class and a few kids looked at me in a funny manner. I made a wise-crack pretending nothing had happened hoping people wouldn't think I was weird. It felt awkward. The teacher asked me if I was okay, and I lied telling her I was fine. I made an excuse about being worried he got sick on my jacket. She squinted at me like she didn't believe me. I reassured her it was true, reluctantly returning to my seat. I didn't want to look like a crazy kid, so I had to pretend everything was okay and act as normal as possible.

I performed the breathing ritual as I approached my desk. The janitor was cleaning up the sickness on the floor. I felt relieved I didn't have to deal with the physical throw up next to me. But for the remainder of the day, I contemplated whether or not the air had been contaminated by his sickness and what the odds were I may 'catch it'. I also kept a close eye on every student making sure no one 'looked' sick. If anyone got out of their seat to go to the back of the room, I would feel the heat in my neck and need to count breaths to calm down. I didn't want anyone to know I was doing this, so I made sure I was acting as normally as possible. Even when the bad feelings happened, I made sure my face stayed neutral and normal. When my classmates asked me what happened earlier, I made jokes about how gross Jeff was and how I wanted to get away from him. For some reason, everyone bought my lies. I felt terrible for being mean about Jeff, but I didn't know any other way to excuse what really happened.

Using breathing techniques and monitoring student's faces for signs they looked sick or not helped me through the rest of the day. I also repeated prayers to God asking that no one else throw up. I apologized profusely to God for whatever I must have done wrong to make this happen. I reasoned good things happen to good people, and bad things happen to bad people. So, I had to believe God must be punishing me for something bad I had done. Why had I not felt anything like this before? Maybe I had done something deserving this harsh punishment? I prayed for forgiveness repeatedly hoping God would hear me, be merciful, and take this away.

The bell rang and I felt relieved to get out of the classroom. I was mentally exhausted. That classroom had felt like a prison. I had afterschool program before mama picked me up, but at least I was far away from the throw up air. I met my friends at our usual spot in the cafeteria for roll call and announcements. As all the students began to file in, I didn't feel I had enough time to look at everyone's face to make sure no one looked sick. There were too many kids to track and the bad feelings began again. Was the room big enough so if someone threw up, I wouldn't be near the bad air? Could I get out of here easily if someone throws up near me? What if there is a virus going around? What if I cannot get away? *Start the breathing ritual, Chrissie. You can control this in 6 breaths.*

My friend Dani looked at me quizzically and asked if I was okay. I must have looked panicked. *Dang it, I don't want anyone to know!* I quickly put a 'normal' face on making a quick excuse to cover up. She didn't seem to buy it, but I concentrated on looking normal and tried distracting her with a joke. I started the breathing ritual and prayed to God no one would throw up this afternoon. I bargained with God, telling Him I would be the best Christian I could possibly be as long as He would not let someone throw up near me.

We filed out of the cafeteria onto the playground and I started feeling the hot, tingly feeling for so many reasons I couldn't keep up with them. Everywhere I looked, I would see reasons for bad feelings. Someone ran past me and I worried they were sprinting to the bathroom. Someone bent over and I feared they were heaving and throwing up. Kids were spinning on the tire swing and I worried they might get dizzy and throw up. Kids ran toward the teachers' chairs and I worried they were asking to go to the bathroom to throw up.

I was hypervigilant and suspicious of anyone possibly throwing up. I constantly checked kid's faces, breathing my six breaths, and praying to God. I did all of this while managing to keep it a secret from my friends. No one suspected anything. I wanted desperately to tell someone, but I was afraid they would think I was stupid. I was also scared saying it out loud would prove it was real. I wanted to believe this was temporary. I wanted to believe whatever I did to offend God, I could remedy it with prayer and He'd take it away. I couldn't imagine things could change so drastically and quickly without a reason. Maybe it was just a bad day. Maybe I did something wrong and just need to remedy it. Maybe this would all be gone tomorrow.

My stomach had been in knots all day from stress. When the bad feelings began, I was unable to decipher whether they were just the bad feelings or if it was a sign I was going to throw up. They felt very similar. I was in a constant state of anxiety trying to figure out if what I was feeling were bad feelings or actual stomach/throw up feelings. I would feel temporary relief when the breathing ritual worked because it proved I wasn't going to throw up. But each time it would surface, I'd feel the doubt of what if this time you really are going to throw up? It was confusing and exhausting, but I engaged every time to prove it was or wasn't me actually getting sick.

My last friend left afterschool program around 4:45. I couldn't believe I fooled them into thinking I was fine. I had spent every moment today in this stupid thought process, but was able to maintain 'normal' Chrissie to everyone. I was relieved to wave goodbye to her because I was so exhausted from the façade I was compelled to put on. I sat alone on the swings. I put my face against the chain, breathing in the metallic smell that had rubbed off on my hands. I dropped my face down and felt the cold chain link hit the inside of my mouth. I tasted metal. My head popped up in panic. I just had my hands all over the chain and now it was in my mouth.

What if there are throw up germs on the chain from other people's hands and now they are in my mouth? What if I swallowed someone's germs who may get sick tonight or tomorrow and now I am contaminated? What if there were throw up germs on MY hands and I just got them in my mouth?

I spit saliva on the ground and wiped the inside of my mouth with my clothes trying to get the germs out of my mouth. My stomach dropped and I felt a strong urge to go to the bathroom. The tingling started in my neck and I began walking fast toward the teacher. *Oh my God, I have the throw up sickness. It's happening right now. My breathing counts won't help. This is for real. I'm going to really throw up.* I didn't want to run because I worried running would prove I was really going to throw up and I wanted to believe it wasn't real. If I walk, maybe it will prove I really don't have to throw up and it isn't urgent. My breathing rituals went past six breaths without calming me down, and I worried it was 'proof' this time I was really going to throw up.

I quickened my pace while grabbing the bathroom pass. I could smell the metal from my hands and with every whiff, the hot feeling in my neck reminded me I had ingested germs which may or may not be throw up germs. I pulled open the school door quickly rounding the corner to the bathroom. I bolted into one of the concrete stalls. I couldn't close and lock the door fast enough. I had to go to the bathroom badly and was terrified it was because I was getting sick from ingesting throw up germs from the swing. I tugged on my overlapped cloth belt stuck in the metal loop at every angle, but couldn't get it loose. I hated these belts because I could never figure out how to get them undone. I pulled furiously at the loose end, but it wouldn't budge. The anxiety was overwhelming, and sweat was running down my face. *Isn't this physical 'proof' something is really wrong and it isn't just bad thoughts?* I started crying and screaming at my belt. My desperate screams echoed off the tall, concrete stalls. I prayed out loud no one would hear me in the hallway.

It was too late. I couldn't hold it any longer. I grabbed the side of the concrete wall knowing I pooped my pants because of my stupid belt. I sobbed uncontrollably. I finally ripped the belt off, yanking my pants down completely embarrassed for myself. I undressed shamefully. I threw my undies in the trash and cleaned up as best as I could. The front of my t-shirt was soaked with tears. I put my pants back on and looped the stupid cloth belt together. I didn't want to face anyone. What kind of 8 year old poops her pants? Did this mean I really am sick? Does this mean I will get sick? What is happening to me? Everything made sense this morning. Why did my whole life change in one instant? What did I do to deserve this? Will anything be normal again?

I was riddled with fear, anxiety, and exhaustion. Nothing made sense anymore. I wanted to go back to yesterday. I wanted to be somebody different. I wanted this horrible day to be over. I wanted to be normal Chrissie again. I leaned back heavily against the concrete wall and slid down until my bottom hit the cold floor. I wrapped my arms around my knees and wept into my shirt.

What did I do to deserve this? What kind of person am I? What if this never goes away? I can't live like this. I don't want to live like this.

My watch read 5:20pm and I knew mama would arrive at any moment. I couldn't wait to see her, but I didn't want her to see me like this. I wanted her to hold me. I wanted to smell her perfume and remember how things used to be before today. I wanted to tell her everything so she could make it okay, but I knew I couldn't. She would be ashamed of me for thinking these stupid thoughts. She would be ashamed because I pooped my pants. She would be embarrassed if she knew she had a daughter who was such a horrible person with bad thoughts and bad feelings. She would be ashamed if she knew I was such a bad person God had to punish me this way. Also, she probably wouldn't believe me. I could barely believe it myself. I had become a different person in the blink of an eye. I feared my life would never be the same. The Chrissie who existed yesterday was no longer here. There was a new, horrible, and miserable Chrissie. I hated this Chrissie. I wanted the old Chrissie back.

I pulled myself up begrudgingly, washed my face, and slowly walked back to the playground. Mama was waiting for me. A feeling of relief came over me. I wanted to run to her and have her hold me while I cried. I wanted her to reassure me it would be okay. But, I couldn't. Instead, I forced a smile, quickened my stride toward her, and prepared myself to pretend I had a great day.

Chapter 3: The Rituals

I stayed calm, not disclosing anything to mama or my sister Joy about what had happened today. Home felt safe. I was away from the throw up germs and bad thoughts. The temporary relief was intoxicating. Maybe it was just a bad day? Maybe I will wake up tomorrow and this will be gone? Maybe I made it all up? Maybe it was just a fluke? My comfort level at home made me doubt the bad feelings had even happened. There is no way I could have those bad thoughts again after the reassurance I felt now.

I couldn't help wondering why today happened. Whatever had occurred I knew was 'bad' and somehow I caused it. I must have done something bad to deserve this. I couldn't think of anything I had done in particular to make God so angry with me. Maybe if I was more devoted and obedient to God, He would forgive me and take the thoughts away. If I stuck to this plan, maybe He would protect me from throwing up and experiencing bad feelings.

I said a long, detailed, and extensive prayer before bed. I made sure I was thankful for everything good in my life and asked forgiveness for anything I could even stretch my mind to believe was a sin. I named each person in my life I was thankful for to God. At the end of my prayer, I asked God to please not let anyone the ages of 1-114 throw up for the next 24 hours. I figured the oldest person in the world was probably over 100 but not 115. I thought it would be more effective if I counted out the numbers from 1 to 114. I noted the time on my digital clock so I would know if my prayer was answered 24 hours later. I worried maybe I hadn't clearly stated all the ages, so I counted to 114 again. I noted the new time on my clock knowing I had to have my prayer done the next night by the exact time to be protected. This would mean I needed to start early tomorrow night in case I made any mistakes or didn't get the prayer right before time lapsed.

I felt confident in my plan. I trusted God would see how detailed, devoted, and serious I was about not having bad thoughts. I hoped I had done enough to convince God I deserved a second chance.

The next morning I opened my eyes to a new day. My confidence from last night was shattered when I sat up. The bad thoughts about throwing up plagued me as soon as my feet hit the floor. The thought of being in the classroom made me feel the hot feelings in my neck and chest. They felt worse today than yesterday. I dropped to my knees, praying to God to save me from this. I started my breathing ritual and prayed silently. Nothing was working. My breathing increased and my stomach felt upset and weird. This had to be a definite sign I was going to get sick if I went to school. Why would I react this way if there wasn't any truth behind it? Why would my body physically react if these thoughts weren't true?

Mama came into my room and I told her I was sick. She felt my forehead. Her hands were so cold. I hoped my forehead was hot enough to convince her I needed to stay home. She saw right through my lie. She told me to get up and get ready. I started crying and panicking. She got the thermometer. I stuck it in my mouth praying I had a fever so I could stay home. *Why is God doing this to me? I promised I would do everything right. What did I do between last night and this morning to offend Him?*

Mama checked the thermometer. It was 98.5 degrees, so I had no way out. I pulled myself together and made a pact with God. I promised I would keep up the prayers and I would do everything from now on to be the best person and Christian I could possibly be. I begged Him to accept my plea and never allow me to feel that way again. I knew I could keep up my end of the bargain. If I slipped and did something bad, I accepted God would punish me with the bad feelings and thoughts. All I had to do was to make sure I was the 'perfect' and most devout Christian possible and it would be okay. I felt temporary reassurance with this plan. It made me feel false control. I had to cling to something hopeful otherwise I didn't know how I would make it through today.

As I entered school, I was hyper-vigilant about my body and my breathing. If I could stay ahead of the bad feelings, I may have a chance at neutralizing them with breathing and prayer rituals. Every step closer to my classroom made the tingling in my neck and arms increase. I fought back with prayers and breathing at every step. I wanted to run away from there, but I knew if I did not go into the classroom now I'd never be able to. I felt confident in my pact with God. The breathing ritual worked a high percentage of the time, which convinced me I had a good chance of avoiding the bad thoughts and feelings through the day.

My confidence was shattered as I walked around the corner and saw Jeff in his seat. *What is he doing here? Why would his parents let him come back? There is no way he is well enough to be here. What if he is still sick and is going to spread it to all of us? How could the teacher let him back in the classroom? How could God do this to me? What did I do to Him to deserve this kind of punishment? Why did God hate me so much? I hate Jeff! I hate my teacher! I hate everyone in the classroom who doesn't care that Jeff is back today! I hate this school! I HATE MYSELF AND MY LIFE!*

I didn't want anyone to see me freak out. I held my breath as I walked into the classroom and focused on praying when I walked past Jeff's seat. I couldn't look at him and I didn't want to breathe any air near him. I bolted to my seat, gasping out loud in desperation. The boy sitting next to me heard the gasp and gave me a weird look. I returned the weird face trying to make a joke about it. I couldn't look at the spot where the throw up had been yesterday. Just thinking about it made me feel I couldn't breathe. I didn't want to look at Jeff, but oddly wanted to keep an eye on him to make sure he wasn't still sick. I wondered how everyone in the room was okay with him being back. How was everyone so calm? I began worrying someone else may throw up today since he had spread throw up germs all over the classroom yesterday and today. I needed to be vigilantly in control of every person in the room. I could never really know who was going to throw up, but I could be prepared in advance in case I needed to escape. I started right away. I worked my way from the back of the room examining each person's face.

Do they look happy? Do they look sick? Do they look pale or overheated? Is their head down?

If anyone looked like something was wrong, I would keep an eye on them until I could prove otherwise. There were several students with expressions that didn't seem right to me. I watched them intently until I was reassured I had made a mistake. If someone smiled or laughed, I assumed they weren't sick. So, I needed to do anything I could to make people who felt threatening smile or laugh.

There was a girl in the back with her head down. This worried me. There was only one way to know for sure. I got up and slowly approached the back of the room with a pencil needing to be sharpened. I had to keep safe breathing distance from her in case she had the throw up germs. A couple desks before hers, I pretended to slam my foot against a desk rail and started laughing loudly. Her head popped up. I looked quickly at her, searching her face for any kind of indication she was sick. She yawned, rubbed her eyes like she was just tired, and put her head back down. The student whose desk I kicked made fun of me, and I continued to the pencil sharpener. I was relieved. She didn't seem sick, just tired. I believed everyone in the classroom was in the clear, so I felt momentarily reassured.

I did this ritual all day. I figured there were periods when individuals may be more inclined to get sick. Early in the day after breakfast and the first two hours after lunch were dangerous times. These were 'observation' times. I was careful to make sure no one thought I was acting weirdly or staring at them. The last thing I wanted was for anyone to suspect I was doing this. How would I explain wanting to find out if someone thought they may or may not throw up anytime soon? If I suspected someone was sick, I would get as close as possible to them without being exposed to their germs and try to get them to move around or talk to get a better assessment.

I was nervous about going back to class after lunch. The hot, tingly feelings in my neck and head were in overdrive on the walk to the classroom. I made sure to count my breaths, say my prayer rituals, and assess everyone's face as we walked down the hallway. Once the clock chimed at 1pm, I felt relief. It had been twenty-four hours since Jeff threw up and neither I nor anyone in the classroom had become sick. I figured the danger of getting sick would be within the first twenty-four hours after exposure. However, I figured there was an incubation period for sicknesses. I had no idea what it was for Jeff's sickness, so I guessed I would be safe after seventy-two hours. This meant if I had not thrown up by Sunday at 1pm, I would be in the clear and wouldn't have to worry anymore about catching his sickness. Waiting another forty-eight hours seemed daunting, but at least I would be home and away from Jeff and this classroom. I had so much hope I would be okay because I made it through the first twenty-four hours, but I didn't want to jinx it. So I stuck to the seventy-two hour rule and maintained rituals every moment.

I was relieved when the bell rang and it was time to go to afterschool program. I had successfully controlled the throw up situation in my classroom all day. However, it was harder keeping up with rituals when more kids were involved. I didn't know everyone at afterschool program and felt overwhelmed trying to keep on top of everyone's mood. I staked out areas on the playground I felt were safe. The swings and the monkey bars felt safe. There was no way I was ever going near the tire swings. That was a breeding ground for barfing. I measured my parameters and decided which areas were threatening and which were not. When my friends questioned me about not wanting to go to specific areas, I responded with a weird 'better than them' attitude about which areas were 'cool' and which were not. I could hardly believe some of the things I said to them, but it worked. I felt terrible for being deceitful and worried God would punish me for acting like this. I justified it by reassuring myself about the abundance of forgiveness I would ask for later. I believed my behavior was a necessity to avoid the bad thoughts and feelings. I had to control everything and everyone possible in order to protect myself from the bad thoughts and feelings.

It was 5:30pm and I saw mama walk through the doors. I ran and grabbed her around her waist. It was such a different feeling to see her today compared to yesterday. I was sick and exhausted yesterday. Today, I felt like I had a working plan against the evil in my mind. I was so happy mama was taking me away from school for a whole weekend. I wasn't in the clear until Sunday at 1pm, but at least I would be safe at home and minimizing the threats.

It had been a successful day. I neither saw anyone throw up nor did I feel exposed to anyone with throw up germs. I needed to solidify exactly what I had done the night before and this morning. If I repeated everything the exact way I had done before, I could replicate this success every day. I now had a standard formula I could follow for success to assure I wouldn't be exposed to or experience the bad thoughts or feelings. What a relief! I could control this as long as I was constantly vigilant.

Every day I need to do everything exactly how I did it last night and this morning. Every day I need to be the best Christian I possibly can so God doesn't have to punish me. This is the way to control this. This is the way to not suffer.

I believed I was strong enough to handle it. This was my new way of life. One-hundred-percent vigilance and one-hundred-percent commitment would win against the bad thoughts. I believed I could do it. I could beat this every day. I may not like it, but this was the Chrissie I would have to be in order to survive this.

Chapter 4: Who is Chrissie?

No one suspected anything was different about me since the bad thoughts happened. I was spending hours in daily rumination, avoidance, and prayer rituals. But I was also becoming an expert in masking them. There were two different sides of Chrissie. There was the internal, anxiety-riddled, ritualistic Chrissie and the outward 'everything is just great' Chrissie. However confusing it felt, I sensibly kept the two separate. I had insight that my behavior and intense worry didn't make sense, but what stopped me from seeking help was the voice in my head saying "if there was not some truth to this, you wouldn't worry about it." This voice kept me silent. This voice held me in fear.

I had been socially outgoing before the bad thoughts showed up, so trying to keep them hidden pushed me into being the center of attention. I wanted everyone to see, know, and believe in the fun, normal Chrissie. If I created a big enough persona on the outside, no one would suspect the bad things happening on the inside. What would everyone think if they knew I was such a horrible person that God had to punish me when I did wrong? Wouldn't my family and friends despise me if they knew what a disappointment I was to God? No one else got punished when they sinned, so I must be so despicable that God needed to deliberately punish me. I didn't want my family and friends to see the evil person I must be in God's eyes. I believed I could manage it enough so no one would ever see the truth. I would do whatever was needed to please God in order to stave off these punishments.

I believed I controlled throw up threats with prayers, breathing, counting hours after exposures, and face observations. But every so often, I assumed I was not vigilant enough or had done something to offend God because I would experience bad thoughts and feelings again. I equated this to believing God was angry with me. I prayed every night for God's tests and trials to stop. I begged for a pure heart and a new beginning to make things right. Every morning I awoke hoping the bad thoughts and feelings would disappear as a result of my devotion. But every morning I woke, still feeling the horrible feelings, thoughts, and misery, wondering what I had done to deserve God's wrath. I believed I was doing something wrong for God not to trust me or believe I was a good person. I lived in an exhausting cycle.

Rationally, I saw some cracks in my theory on God being the superpower controlling my thoughts and actions. It didn't make sense why I would become caught in a ruminative and depressive cycle when I could think of nothing I had done wrong. I would scour my memory for potential sins, but found myself saying prayers of forgiveness for things I didn't believe were sinful, hoping it would provide reprieve. I was so desperate for relief, I was buying the idea everything I did or didn't do was worthy of punishment. While vaguely understanding it was nonsensical from a worldly perspective, my brain convinced me it was the only way to control it. In reality, I had no leverage with a higher power, no way of confirming my theory was correct or incorrect, and no foreseeable way of ending this cycle. Yet, I continued to perform the rituals in hopes something miraculous would occur to make everything okay. Maybe God would recognize my vigilance and reward me by letting me wake up one morning to find all this was over and gone. I clung to this hope every single day.

My avoidance rituals became more prevalent as I developed areas and people deemed 'off limits'. Just as I set parameters at the playground the first ritual day, I identified areas of school I considered 'contaminated' with throw up germs. I avoided the janitorial staff. They were in the direct line of throw up exposure because they had to clean it up. They were off limits within 20 feet of exposure. If I saw a janitor, I would turn immediately and go around the school if necessary to avoid being exposed. If I knew of an area kids had thrown up, I avoided those places for good. If I was forced to go into a 'contaminated' bathroom I would inspect the stalls, hold my breath for as long as possible, or breathe through my shirt if needed.

If anyone in my classroom threw up, I isolated them from me and my friends. I would do everything I could to ostracize them. I felt awful for doing this, but couldn't risk their germs being near me. I reasoned if they throw up once, they may throw up again forcing me into the seventy-two hour countdown which I deemed the most torturous ritual. If I found out a kid had thrown up, I decided to neither be friends nor associate with them. As a precaution, I could not risk them being part of my life. It wasn't fair, but seemed the most effective solution.

However, this avoidance ritual was tricky. When people I cared about threw up, I found myself in a convoluted situation. I would have to decide which was more important, the rituals or the individual. Socially, I had to make some tough decisions.

One evening, my best friend Allison came over after school to spend the night. We were playing outside at my neighbor's house, laughing, and having a great time. As we walked back to the house, she said "This is so much fun, I feel so good!" The hot and tingly feeling started to creep up in my neck. *Why would she say she feels good? Is that going to jinx something? That is tempting fate! I wish she had never said that!*

I became quiet and she asked if something was wrong? I was busy asking forgiveness from God for thinking about how she would just assume she felt good and wouldn't throw up. *How could anyone just say out loud that they feel good? Don't they know by saying that they are seriously asking for trouble?* I did my best to blow off her inquiry and pretended nothing was wrong. But I became absorbed in rituals for the next couple hours.

While watching TV in the living room after dinner, she quickly got up to go to the bathroom. It was weird she didn't say anything before she left. I started feeling the hot, tingly feeling on my neck. *What if she is throwing up because of what she said earlier today? Why would she be so stupid to say that and now she is going to be sick and expose me to being sick? I hate her. Why did I ask her to come over?*

I strained my neck as close to the bathroom as I could at a distance safe enough to prevent exposure just in case. I heard her cough and I began panicking. I wanted to run out of the house, but needed to stay and not panic in front of mama and Joy. The toilet flushed once...then twice...then three times. *Dear God, I am so sorry she said that. I didn't do anything---it was her. Why aren't you punishing HER instead of ME?*

A few minutes later, she came out of the bathroom looking pale. I backed into the corner of the room at a 'safe' distance, preparing to hear the worst. She asked my mom to call her parents because she had thrown up. I wanted to scream! *WHY WOULD YOU BE SO STUPID TO SAY YOU FELT GOOD? ARE YOU A STUPID IDIOT?* I couldn't look at her. She walked toward me and I quickly moved to the other side of the room. I didn't say I was sorry she was sick. I wasn't sorry. I hated her. She had said those stupid words and now I was being punished. Now, everything in my house was contaminated with her throw up germs. How was I going to make it through the next seventy-two hours? I couldn't look her in the face. She gathered her stuff, while I sat across the room never uttering a word. There was a knock at the door. Allison stood up, looked back at me, and said she was sorry she got sick. I stared at the wall and didn't respond.

I knew I was being a jerk, but I didn't care. How could she do this to me? Everything in my house was now unsafe for seventy-two hours. I had nowhere to go. Weekends were my refuge from the contamination of school, and now I had lost an entire weekend of

24

solace because of her. She callously referred to herself as 'feeling good' and now I was screwed. I wanted nothing to do with her anymore. She had been my best friend for years, and she had just ruined the friendship.

The rest of the weekend was agony. I barely slept from vigilantly watching if I was going to be sick. Any twinge in my stomach sent panic up my spine about this possibly being the time I caught her illness. I had to stave off panic almost every hour. Allison called several times telling me she was sorry and feeling better, but I refused to talk to her. My mom was puzzled, but I told her I would talk to Allison at school on Monday so she wouldn't suspect anything. But I didn't want to talk to her on Monday. How was I supposed to see her and act like everything was okay? She was contaminated now and had exposed me! I never wanted to be around her again. She was now dangerous and a threat.

On Monday, Allison approached me in the hallway and I pretended I didn't see her, bolting away. I felt horrible. How could I do this to my best friend? I wanted to be her friend, but how could I now? I avoided her all day. I knew she felt terrible about becoming sick, but I couldn't care. She seemed confused, and it hurt me to ignore her. I wanted to tell her. I wanted to let her know what was going on, but I couldn't. She'd never understand.

Unfortunately, I could think of no way to avoid her at afterschool program. I waited until the last minute to get to the cafeteria so there would be no opportunity to talk before roll call. She smiled at me as I walked up. I half smiled and sat at the other end of the table. I saw her disappointment. It hurt me to be so mean, but I had to choose between battling Allison or the bad thoughts. I knew which battle was easier to win. I ignored her during roll call and announcements. I didn't walk with her to the playground, and I made sure we were never near each other more than 3-5 feet throughout afterschool program. She sensed my animosity and I noticed my other friends were treating her badly because of me as well. They followed my lead. I was grateful, but I hated how it probably made Allison feel.

At one point I looked over and noticed she was on the swings by herself with her head down. She looked sad. I wanted to tell her how sorry I was, but it was her fault for throwing up. I wanted to tell her I didn't make the other girls treat her badly, they were just acting that way because of me. She was my best friend and I wanted to be nice, but I couldn't give in. I wouldn't give in. It was too important to stick to what I knew in my mind I needed to do. I didn't want to risk the alternative.

Her parents picked her up at 4:15. I watched her mom pause after looking at our group, hugging her tight before they walked out the doors. I wasn't sure, but it looked like Allison was crying. I felt sick with guilt. I wanted nothing more than to stay friends with her. But I couldn't have her be more important than my rituals. If she only knew the suffering it would cause me if I let my guard down again, she'd understand. I couldn't risk being exposed again.

I ignored her for a week. She barely talked to us at afterschool program and each day it hurt me so badly. I was treating her horribly because of this stupid fear. After a week, my anxiety waned when I would see or get near Allison. It had been well past seventy-two hours and I wondered if it would be okay to be friends again. The following Monday I talked to her, keeping my distance. I made a stupid excuse about why I had ignored her last week so she wouldn't think it had anything to do with her throwing up. She was happy things were back to normal. But I knew the impact of her throwing up had damaged our friendship. I would never be able to be close to her again. I couldn't feel safe around her. What if she threw up again? I couldn't trust her anymore.

It was difficult deciphering between who I wanted to be versus who I had to be to maintain rituals. I couldn't rationalize why this was happening to me. I obviously had offended God badly to deserve this life. I didn't know what else to do except adhere to the rules and regulations of my monstrous obsession. I was in constant turmoil questioning the validity of my experience because it seemed so ridiculous to worry about this all the time. But, I would get pulled into the cycle by the voice in my head saying "if there wasn't some sort of truth to this, you wouldn't have to do the rituals." The voice kept me trapped. It kept me silent. It kept me miserable. It kept me from having a normal and enjoyable childhood.

It was painful going through this alone. The times I was exposed and triggered were paralyzing. The feeling of anxiety was so overwhelming I felt the need to do anything possible to avoid it. When I would experience anxiety, it was as if I would leave the normal 'Chrissie' body. Hyper-vigilance was paramount to moving through the anxiety. I would become acutely aware of my surroundings and time seemed to slow down. The panic kept me hyperaware every second with no escape. I was paranoid. I couldn't trust anything. I doubted everything. The fear of being exposed to throwing up was so terrifying at times that death seemed like a craved relief. I spent every waking moment seeking out opportunities to avoid throwing up. My world was encapsulated in what to do and not to do in order to avoid my obsession. It was paralyzing and frightening.

I wanted to tell my mom and dad, but I was terrified to say it out loud. My brain was locked into believing if I admitted it out loud it would prove to be real. Saying it out loud would confirm its validity.

I desperately wanted to believe one day I would wake up from this nightmare and life would be normal again. But each ritual-filled passing day convinced me this was my life now and there was no escape.

Where I once loved life and being part of it, I now despised living within it. I hated who I now was. I hated the person I knew I had to be to maintain balance and peace with God. It seemed impossible. I had lost touch with everything good and positive. I had no idea who I was. I could not imagine a time I would be able to experience the Chrissie I had once known.

I believed she was gone forever.

Chapter 5: Baiting Obsessions

I managed the throw up obsession by staying dedicated to daily rituals. It wasn't uncommon to engage in ritualistic behavior every minute. I became an expert at keeping this secret from everyone. The majority of days, I had minimal reason to believe I had been exposed to the obsession and believed this was a direct result of my compliance and dedication to God and my rituals. If I wasn't exposed, God must be pleased with me. However when exposed to throwing up, my world would freefall in a downward spiral of hopelessness and self-deprecation.

Exposure was paralyzing and exhausting. When exposed, I felt frozen. I couldn't think or feel. It was as if time stopped for me, but everyone else kept moving. Every hair stood up on my body like small antennas looking for clues to remedy the overwhelming uncertainty. I would hone in on what and why it was happening, and how to escape without becoming contaminated. I walked a fine line between needing to know for certain if or why someone was sick, and how to stay far enough away to keep from being contaminated. I had an incredible ability to engage in things around me while zeroing in on a trigger elsewhere so no one suspected anything. After a severe trigger, I would be exhausted from the intense anxiety. Then I had to worry what I had done wrong to make God mad. I had to pray for hours in hope of figuring out what I needed forgiveness for. My guilt and shame for making God angry was just as intense as the fear of my obsession.

After major triggers, I would feel periods of intense sadness and hopelessness. I would feel shame and guilt for how bad a person I must be to deserve these punishments. They felt like waves of depression, but I held on hoping the sadness would break and I'd feel 'normal' again. Each time, I counted the days and weeks I felt this way, making a mental note of the length. I dared not write it down. If

I wrote down anything pertaining to this fear and anxiety, it proved it was real. I used the length of times as a scale with which to compare upcoming waves of sadness. As long as I had a time frame by which to measure, I could hope the bad times would always break and I could return to just doing rituals without the sadness.

I became a master at hiding the times I experienced high anxiety and depressive states. I had excuses for escaping situations which could possibly present a threat. I prepared in advance how to exit situations if bad thoughts arose unexpectedly. I was an expert at perfecting the persona of happiness to the outside world, even in the midst of the agonizing torment in my inner world. It was a necessity. I could never let anyone know how often God punished me.

The deeper I became engrossed in the deceit, the more entrenched I became adhering to absolute secrecy about my alternate life. I lost hope in the idea I may wake up one day to find this was gone. I knew this was my life and I had to deal with it. But, it was imperative no one ever find out this secret, or it would be disastrous. It was clear I was on the receiving end of God's wrath. When I am a good person, God rewards me by withholding the bad thoughts and feelings. When I am a bad person, God punishes me by exposing me to threats and triggers. My punishment was the length of time I endured the depressive states as a reminder from God how ashamed He was of me. It made sense to me. I didn't like it, but I didn't believe I had a choice.

I often wondered if everyone else had this type of relationship with God. Why doesn't anyone talk about it? I constantly wished I was anyone other than me, but then worried I may offend God by not appreciating my life. So I spent days repenting in hopes of avoiding punishment. I believed every thought was subject to His punishment or praise. I attempted to monitor every thought engaging in a constant state of repentance for thoughts I worried may be punishable. Just when I would believe I had done things the right way, I would be exposed to throwing up or someone who had thrown up. The cycle would begin again.

As I moved into my teenage years, there were times I seemed to have a handle on my thoughts and rituals. Weeks would go by without significant triggers. I was grateful, thanking God for His mercy because I knew in a second I could be brought to my knees in fear. But, I started to notice bad feelings could happen with other bad thoughts. A perceived bad thought would enter my mind and my body would start to react the same way as when I thought about throwing up. This alarmed and confused me. Was God transferring punishment onto something else?

One evening, I was babysitting and watching 'The Exorcist'. I had no idea what the movie was about before I began watching. I was completely devastated at the imagery and content on demon possession. I was too paralyzed to move despite my intense anxiety and fear. I worried about touching the TV to turn it off. If I did, does that prove I'm denying demon possession could happen? Will I be susceptible for denying it? I forced myself to watch the entire movie, hoping that in the end there would be a happy outcome.

I was sorely disappointed. I felt riddled with guilt and anxiety about willingly watching a movie about the devil. But I had been too frightened of the consequences of turning it off. I knew God was going to punish me even though I didn't know anything about it and had been too scared to turn it off.

The bad feelings engulfed me immediately following the credits. I felt paralyzed. I wished I could go back two hours before and stop myself from watching it. For the next month, I obsessively engaged in prayer rituals and repentance. My radar was fixated on good and evil. I felt I had promoted evil by watching the movie. I feared God would abandon me. I couldn't sleep. I stopped eating. I worried my soul was tainted from watching a movie promoting the devil. My thoughts became a holy battleground on whether or not I sided with good or evil.

I was suspicious about my similar physical reaction between fear of the devil and the fear of throwing up, but I couldn't put my finger on how they were related. When I thought about evil and Satan, my neck and head became hot and tingly. My breathing would increase, my chest would tighten, and my hands and arms would go numb. I had no choice other than to rationalize God was causing this reaction. If I had the bad physical symptoms, I must have done something wrong to deserve them. Obviously watching the movie was 'wrong' in God's eyes and He needed to punish me. The punishment lasted for a month before it finally dissipated.

In 8th grade, I went on spring break to Panama City beach with a friend and her family. As they packed the car to drive back to Georgia, I watched her younger cousin throw a stuffed animal, hitting her sister in the face. I jumped up to see if she was okay. She paused for a second before her face became grossly distorted and screaming and crying ensued. The face she made looked hilarious and I began to chuckle. Then my neck became hot and I quickly stifled my laughter. My breathing began to increase. I jumped out of the car walking as fast as I could away from the girls. I didn't want to hear the girl crying anymore. *Why in the world would I laugh at a child who was crying? What kind of person laughs at pain? Do I think harming children is funny? Do I want her to cry to get a good laugh? Am I going to harm her on the way home just so I can laugh at her?*

I bent over, shaking my head vigorously. *How was I going to ride in this car the entire way home with these feelings? Is this the kind of a person I am?* I prayed to God for forgiveness for whatever I had done to deserve this bad thought. *How could I be punished this way?*

What did I do to deserve the bad thought of taking pleasure in the pain of kids?

I would have to sit next to this girl in her car seat for an eight hour drive home. I was terrified. *What if I do something to cause her pain on purpose so I can laugh at her? What if I want her to get hurt so I can take pleasure in it?* I heard my friend calling out to me. I needed to pretend everything was okay. I walked to the car refusing to look at the little girls in case I thought I wanted to hurt them to make myself laugh. I pulled my legs into the backseat, put my headphones on, and stared out the window.

I spent the next eight hours avoiding the girls. I worried I would look at them and laugh. I worried I had somehow turned into a child abuser that day. It didn't make sense. I knew I didn't want to hurt the girl. I would never intentionally hurt anyone. But, my head told me if it wasn't a possibility, I would have never thought about it in the first place. This thought caused anxiety every time it arose. The hot, tingly feeling in my neck recurred when the girls spoke or when anyone would say their names. I wanted to escape the car so badly, but I was trapped for hours. I channeled the strength to stave off emotion for eight hours. I focused intently on my breathing and prayers.

I wanted to burst into tears when I saw my house in the distance. I was exhausted from hours of managing the physical feelings and bad thoughts. I barely spoke a word to anyone as I exited the car. I wanted to get as far away from them as possible. I had such a good time on the trip until that day when I saw what kind of horrible person I may now potentially be. I avoided my friend for the next few weeks. Seeing her face reminded me of the terrible person I might become. I prayed forgiveness for whatever I had done to cause God to punish me with such a horrible thought. I prayed God would save me from becoming a child abuser.

After several weeks, the fear began loosening its grip on me. It didn't stick like the throw up fear had. I was relieved when I felt it start to break. I recognized a connection between the child abuse fear, the fear of the devil, and the throw up fear, but I couldn't find a definitive reason. The only thing that made sense to me was that I was a bad person and deserved punishment from God. Wouldn't I just know if it was something else? As long as I was good, God would withhold the bad thoughts. When I sinned in His eyes, He would punish me by making these horrible thoughts appear.

Little did I know, these thoughts and other brushes with obsessions were only baiting me. My brain was being primed. It kept me fearful and vigilant enough to pave the way for the obsession that would finally stick, changing my life forever.

Chapter 6: The Fear that Stuck

By high school, I had created a persona portraying success and near perfection by appearance. Freshman year was new and exciting. I made the cheerleading squad and had no problems making friends. The throw up obsession had taken a back seat to the excitement of high school life. I got triggered now and then, but my rituals were so dialed in I rarely had an episode lasting longer than seventy-two hours. Things felt so good I almost wondered if those years of worrying were a blip on the radar of life. Maybe it had been a phase? Maybe I had proven to God I was a good person so He didn't have to 'test' and 'punish' me anymore? Maybe I would eventually forget about the bad thoughts and feelings and never have to experience them again! Optimism came into my life for the first time since the bad thoughts began.

My freshman year was a whirlwind of new friends and experiences. As it came to a close, cheerleading tryouts began for the sophomore squad. All my teammates were trying out again, so it seemed easy to predict the outcome. I could barely sit still Friday afternoon waiting for the bell to ring to see the posted results. As soon as it rang, I bolted from class to the entryway of the school where the results were posted. I couldn't get to the front to see the list. Girls were screaming in excitement, and I was dying to see who would be on our team. I pushed my way to the front and started reading from the top. I read the names from top to bottom on the JV list, but didn't see my name. What? *Did I make Varsity?* I started from the top to the bottom on the Varsity list, but didn't see 'Chrissie Hodges' anywhere. I looked at the JV list again. Maybe I didn't read it right. But, I reread the list, and sure enough my name was absent. *Did they make a mistake? How could this be? Is there a misprint?* I turned around to face my best friends whose names were on the list. They looked at the floor with no idea what to say to me.

I turned and bolted in complete desperation. I ran to the teachers in charge of the squads and banged on their classroom door. They reluctantly waved me in. I questioned their decision and they confirmed yes, I had not made the team. As soon as I heard those words, I felt myself becoming numb from my head down. I could see their mouths moving, but I couldn't hear anything they were saying. *Is this really happening? How could I have not made the team? I have been a cheerleader for four years! I am good at it! What did I do wrong? What will I do now?*

I couldn't be in the same room with them anymore. I hated them. I always suspected they were shallow, miserable women trying to relive some teenage experience they never had, and this confirmed it for me. I had been superficially nice to them because of being on the team even though I couldn't stand them, and now I realized it was for nothing. I made an excuse before tears started bursting out of my eyes, and ran to the parking lot. My friend Chay came to my rescue. She saw how upset I was and helped me get away from school as fast as possible. We got to her house and I sobbed uncontrollably. I could barely speak. I could barely move. I felt like I had lost my identity. I felt like a failure. I felt afraid and lost.

Later that evening, another friend convinced me I would feel better if we went to the high school baseball game. All I wanted to do was crawl in a hole and feel sorry for myself, but I reluctantly agreed to go. I didn't want to see anyone from school. I wondered if everyone knew I didn't make the squad. I wondered if everyone thought I was a failure. I wondered if they would see how swollen my face was from crying. I wondered if everyone was laughing at me behind my back.

To my surprise, we walked up the bleachers and everyone acted normal. No one judged me, shunned me, or said anything about not making the squad. I was deeply hurt inside, but I opened myself up to socialize putting on the familiar façade of happiness to everyone. And to my surprise, I met a cute guy despite how terrible I felt inside. His name was Chris. I had seen him before, but never talked to him. I thought he was incredible from the moment we started talking. He acted interested in me, which surprised me. I felt completely deflated, yet he was interested in wanting to know more about me. It was a fantastic boost after this agonizing day. It was a blessing to meet and feel excited about something after the terrible loss I felt earlier.

The next few weeks, I began seeing Chris more and was thrilled about it. My feelings for him overshadowed my sadness about not making the cheerleading squad. It was the perfect situation to help me recover from the loss. For the first month, it was a whirlwind of fun and excitement. Chris swept me off my feet and I was ecstatic someone as great as him would be interested in me. I had been smitten with guys prior to him, but this was the first time I could be in a position to actually go on dates. It was a blast and it took my mind completely off my sadness.

After a month, I began to feel bored in the relationship. The newness wore off and I didn't feel excited being with him anymore. I was confused by my feelings. He was fantastic and adorable, but I just didn't feel interested in him anymore. I started to feel a serious crush on another guy, and it made me feel guilty and scared. Chris was so nice to me and treated me well. How could I not appreciate him and wish I was with someone else? I felt like a bad person. Also, Chris was the reason I was okay after not making the cheerleading squad. If I don't have him anymore, would the sad feelings come back? I kept convincing myself I needed to stay with him, but every time I saw him my feelings were becoming less favorable toward the relationship. I wasn't sure what to do. I was scared if I broke up with him, the feelings of sadness would flood in and I wasn't ready for that. I also wasn't sure if the other guy liked me as much as I liked him, so what if

I broke it off with Chris and got rejected? I wasn't sure I could handle that right now. So, I kept things cool even though I wasn't sure I was entirely interested in him anymore.

A few weeks after my relationship with Chris became questionable, I spent the night at a friend's house. We stayed up talking about usual gossip and of course, boys. My friend was smitten with the guy she was seeing and for good reason. He was incredibly hot, funny, and so much fun to be around. I even had a secret crush on him. But, the conversation took an odd turn. The topic of sex came up. She asked me if I had slept with the guy I was seeing. I was appalled. *Of course I haven't slept with him! I cannot imagine the type of punishment I would get from God if I committed THAT sin!!* I nervously laughed and replied I wasn't sure if I was ready to do that. I didn't even want to say the word 'sex' because I was so worried just by talking about it God would punish me. I tried to change the subject, but it wasn't working. I started feeling the bad feelings. I was trapped. She wouldn't stop talking about it and I didn't want her to know how uncomfortable I was, so I just listened. She was trying to tell me something. There was an awkward pause. Hoping to end the conversation immediately, I jokingly said something about what it would be like if we all just did it like it was no big deal. I could not imagine anyone our age would actually have sex because it was so wrong. But, she just responded with a sly smile. I sat in silence feeling more emotions than I could process. "Really?" I asked. She nodded. My jaw dropped.

I felt angry. I couldn't believe it. Why can everyone do whatever they want and not worry about being punished? Am I the only one dealing with a backlash of aftermath when I even suspect I have sinned?

I felt sad. What is so wrong with me that I am unable to do anything without fearing the wrath of punishment being heaped on me? What did I do to deserve this sort of power struggle between myself and my God? How am I worse than everyone else?

I felt jealous. Why can't I be like everyone else and do anything I want without worrying about stupid repercussions of being a bad person?

But mostly, I felt scared. Will I ever be in a place where I don't have to feel guilty for everything I do and worry about my punishment if I do something wrong? What if I am doomed for the rest of my life? What if something happens again and I get sucked back into the bad times? What have I done to offend God in such a way that this is the life I have to lead?

It wasn't fair. She was talking about it, but I could barely hear anything because of the emotional stress I was feeling. I wasn't judging her for having sex. I felt sick no one else had to worry about consequences the way I did. I couldn't understand why it was different for me. *Why me?* I was afraid my friend might suspect my frustration. As soon as I found a place to end the conversation, I made excuses about being tired and headed to the spare bedroom.

I turned out the lights and replayed our conversation in my head. I began to feel the bad physical feelings but couldn't understand why? Was I being punished already for having the conversation? I didn't start it, my friend did! I closed my eyes in effort to think about something else. I visualized the guy I had been seeing and I cringed a little bit. That was it, I cannot see him anymore. I am not into him anymore. I felt more attracted to my friends' boyfriend than my own. I thought about my friend and her boyfriend and how much they must like each other to be able to have sex without consequences. I felt jealous. I wondered if I would ever be able to experience the normal things teenagers and adults do without being afraid.

Suddenly, the jealous feeling was ripped out of my brain and replaced with an explicit visual image of the two of them having sex.

WHOA! NOPE! EW! NO! STOP THINKING THAT! GOD, UGH!

But, as I tried to forget it, the image kept coming back into my mind. It felt stuck. *STOP THINKING ABOUT YOUR FRIENDS HAVING SEX, CHRISSIE!* The harder I tried to stop thinking about the image, the more intense it became. My mind began warping everything I was thinking into questions. *Why can't I stop thinking about my friend having sex? Does that mean I want to have sex with her boyfriend? You can't because she likes him so much?! But, I am attracted to him? Do I want to? NO! You can't do that to her! Stop thinking that!*

My thoughts were racing. The bad feelings began to intensify. I felt as if I couldn't breathe, my neck and head felt hot and tingly, and my arms were feeling numb. I knew God was punishing me for talking about sex. The image was burned in my mind and the questions were spinning out of control. I couldn't figure out why I was reacting this way.

And then it happened.

If you aren't worried about wanting to have sex with her boyfriend, maybe you can't stop thinking about it because of her? What if you are attracted to your friend? Do you like seeing your friend having sex? Since you can't stop thinking about it, does that mean you really like her? Does that mean you are supposed to be gay?

I sat up, gasping for air in a full panic attack. I threw the covers onto the floor and jumped onto my knees. I could barely breathe trying to process the questions in my mind. *What is happening? This isn't true! I don't like my friend, I don't like women! I've always liked men? Am I turning gay? Can people turn gay? But, I don't want to be gay! How can I be gay if I'm not interested in women? Does this mean I have to start liking women now? How can I do this if I just don't like them that way?*

The thoughts were unbearable. I wanted to escape. I wanted to crawl out of the window, running and screaming through the neighborhood. But, I needed to stay quiet. The last person I wanted to see right now was my friend. What if she saw me panicking? What would I tell her? I cannot stop thinking about you having sex with your boyfriend and it may mean I just turned gay. She would think I was nuts! *I THINK I'M NUTS!* None of this makes sense. People just don't turn gay. I knew logically I wasn't gay or didn't want to date women. But, my brain kept saying "well, if there wasn't some truth to it, you wouldn't have thought about it in the first place."

Oh my God. Maybe it can happen. Can it happen? Aren't people born gay? I don't think they spontaneously turn gay?

I thought about my boyfriend to neutralize the thoughts, but it didn't work. I panicked thinking what if the reason I didn't like him anymore was because I had turned gay? *Is this how being gay happens?* I knew there was no way I wanted or could start dating women, so I needed some kind of proof. I tried to flood my brain with thoughts of previous men I had liked. I thought about the guy I had been feeling a crush on lately. I knew how I felt about him was real. How could I turn gay if I have a crush on this guy? I thought about my previous boyfriends and how much I had liked them. Was that not enough proof I liked guys?

Remembering the feelings I had for previous guys gave me a fleeting moment of relief and proof from these weird gay thoughts. I needed to hold onto those feelings to neutralize the bad thoughts. Each time I thought I had enough proof to banish this worry I had turned gay, my brain would tell me because I am so panicked and worried there must be some truth to it. There had to be a logical explanation for this. I rationally knew people didn't 'turn gay' in an instant, especially if they didn't desire the same sex. But, what if I am a rare exception? That thought sent me spiraling into more panic. I don't believe there is anything wrong with being gay, but I just don't want to have to like women! I'm not attracted to women that way!?

I needed to keep focused on finding relief from the thoughts. My urge was to neutralize this fear and somehow prove it wasn't real. I did everything I could every second to answer the questions accurately to disprove the thoughts. It was exhausting. I would feel proof one minute, and then it would vanish. I couldn't keep up with how much doubt I was feeling about whether thoughts were real or whether the feelings I had had were real. I couldn't believe how quickly my life had changed. I wanted to go back to a few hours ago when everything made sense. I wanted to be anyone but myself. I hated myself. I hated this life.

I was baffled why these bad thoughts produced the same physical reaction as the throw up thoughts. It didn't make any sense. How were the two fears related? It seemed too complex to figure out in the midst of my panic, but the curiosity about their connection was nagging at me. I concluded it had to be God's way of punishing me for having the sex conversation. I knew I shouldn't have been talking about it, and I let it happen anyway so God is punishing me for giving in. The throw up fear hadn't been too bad in the last couple of years, so perhaps God needed a new way to punish me.

I recalled the bible passage the 'anti-gay' Christians refer to about how men who lay with men or women who lay with women are sinners, are punished by God for their wrongdoings, and cast down to Hell. I never believed this was true, because I don't believe being gay is sinful, but was this God's way of threatening me if I am not obedient to Him? It seems evil and twisted. I don't believe there is anything morally wrong about being gay, so why would God punish me with these thoughts?

I clasped my hands together tightly. *Dear God, please, please, please forgive me for talking about sex with my friend. I knew it was wrong and I did it anyway. I feared the consequences, and now I know I should have been stronger and better for you. Now I can see what will happen if I am a bad person and Christian and I pray you will take these thoughts away from me. I know I sinned by talking about sex and I will never do it again. Please forgive me, have mercy on me, and do not subject me to this punishment. I will be the best person and Christian I can be, I promise. Please God, have mercy on me. Please make these thoughts go away. I will do anything and everything you need me to do. Please dear God, make this stop. In the name of Jesus Christ, Amen.*

I pulled myself onto the bed, sinking underneath the sheets. The tears began to roll down my face onto the pillow. *I hate my life. I hate who I have to be. I hate this accountability. I hate this burden. I hate I am so horrible of a person to God I have to be punished.*

It felt like fire inside my head from the racing questions why I would worry about something if there wasn't some sort of truth behind it. I concentrated every moment on looking for proof in my past to neutralize each worry. It was exhausting. Just when I believed I could disprove the thoughts, my mind would remind me 'normal non-turning-gay people' would never question anything in the first place. And the cycle would start all over.

I prayed ritualistically. I prayed for sleep. I prayed for forgiveness. I prayed for my soul. I prayed for relief. And, I prayed God would find it in His heart to love me and have mercy on me despite how badly I let Him down.

God granted me a little relief as I finally drifted off to sleep in the early morning hours despite the terror and panic occupying my mind and body. I was too exhausted to fight the thoughts anymore. I prayed this would all be a dream when I woke up the next morning. I prayed it was just a fluke. I prayed I could go back to the Chrissie who existed a few hours before. I prayed she would return in the morning and this would all just be a bad nightmare.

Chapter 7: The Unthinkable

My eyes opened to the sun shining on my face. After a minute, I remembered where I was as my subconscious brain awakened to reality. As I gained conscious thought, the memory of the previous night flashed in my brain. The intrusive thoughts hit me full force. I sat up feeling as if I couldn't get air. My chest was caving in. *Oh no, the thoughts are still there! Oh God, were they real?* My neck and head became tingly. I could barely swallow for the lump in my throat. Someone was walking outside the room. I jumped out of bed, pacing the floor with anxiety.

Calm down, Chrissie. This isn't real. It cannot be real. People don't turn gay overnight. You like guys and have never been attracted to a girl sexually. But, what if it is possible to turn gay overnight? What if I did? But, I don't want to be gay! I don't want to date women! What if I cannot stop thinking about this? Does that mean that I have to be?

I sat down, burying my face in my hands. I tried thinking about the boys I had crushes on to neutralize the bad thoughts. With each attempt, I felt a moment of relief, but the intrusive thoughts quickly returned even more convincingly. *How could I be straight yesterday and gay today? Hadn't I truly liked guys up until now? Had I been pretending? I really liked those guys, didn't I?* I tried to imagine my feelings for them, recalling the sensations of liking them. *Did that prove or disprove I really liked them? What if I would never get to have crushes on guys again because of this? What if I didn't get to date guys again because I turned gay last night and have to date women now?*

I felt I couldn't take this anymore. My body and mind felt out of control. I needed proof right now. How do I get that? Why did I need proof today, when yesterday there was no thought or concern whatsoever about my sexuality? And how could I turn gay if I'm truly not attracted to women?

Okay remember Chrissie, this is what happens when God punishes you. These are bad thoughts and I have done something wrong to deserve them. I need to pray for strength to get through these bad thoughts until I can get back in God's good graces.

Mid-prayer, there was a knock on the door. My friend asked if I was awake. *Oh God, what if I see her and picture her naked? What if I see her and think she is attractive proving I am attracted to her and proving I have to be attracted to women now? Please God make the thoughts go away until I can get home and figure something out.*

I put on a fake, happy face and slowly opened the door. I didn't look at her directly. I worried if I looked at her willingly, it may mean I meant to look at her and that may prove I was attracted to her. She noticed I was being weird and asked if I was okay. I told her I was tired because I didn't sleep well and I wanted to call my mom to pick me up.

"Oh no, I'm sorry you don't feel well. Do you want a hug?" she asked.

"NOOOOOO!" I shouted back. She looked puzzled at my forceful response. I pulled it together and calmly said, "If I am getting sick I don't want to infect you, so no thank you."

"Okay, well you know where the phone is to call your mom. Come up and have breakfast if you feel up to it," she replied.

I shut the door and fell to my knees. How did this happen? Yesterday, I was a heterosexual and today I am afraid I have turned gay? I called mama and told her to hurry and get me because I didn't feel well. I had mixed feelings. I could not wait to see her because I wanted to be near someone who loved me, but I was also scared to see her because what if she knew what was going on in my head? I couldn't tell her what happened. I could never tell anyone. If I said any of this out loud, it might mean I would have to come out of the closet and I didn't believe I was even in the closet.

That moment, I made the decision to never tell anyone this bad thought. If there was ever a time I truly thought I was in the closet and wanted to come out, that would be fine; but as long as I knew I didn't want to be gay but worried I had to, I would keep this to myself. I promised myself there would never be a time or circumstance I would ever disclose this to another human being. I made a pact with myself that I would choose to kill myself before I would tell anyone about this. As soon as I made the decision, a shiver of fear shot down my spine. Something inside of me knew, just as the throw up thoughts had never truly gone away, these wouldn't either. Ever.

This was unimaginable to me. I was terrified.

Chapter 8: Proof or Disproof

Every moment after that evening was a constant engagement in a debate whether or not I had to be gay. It was as if the Chrissie who existed before I went to my friend's house was gone forever. Where did she go? Every day I looked for new ways to 'prove' or 'disprove' the validity of the obsession. When I felt I had mounted enough 'disproof' about the validity, my brain would counter with the idea that worrying about it even once was enough prove otherwise. I would panic, feel like a failure, and have to start over at ground zero. It was an exhausting cycle and a losing battle.

At times I found myself so entrenched in the most ridiculous thoughts about proving or disproving, I would actually question the validity of my behaviors instead of the fear. I would get so lost and overcome with anxiety and worry about things potentially 'proving' the fear was real, while oftentimes recognizing the absurdity in it. My rational mind would take over as if I were coming up for air in the midst of drowning. A rare moment of clarity would surface and I would see how stupid it was to fear something I knew deep down was not true. But the cycle of doubt and fear always pulled me back into the mental compulsions. There was never enough proof, and never enough compulsions to disprove and relieve the anxiety. I craved the times of clarity, but they were far and few between. They had little power over the strength of the obsessions and compulsions. If all opposition to rational thinking failed, my brain would default to *'well if there wasn't some truth to it, you would never have worried about it in the first place'*.

I tried so many things to combat the obsession. I forced myself to think about being with women, which made me feel sick to my stomach. Then I worried I might throw up because I was nauseous so maybe God was doubly punishing me for thinking of being with women. It was painstakingly convoluted. I was at a complete loss how to overcome these two horrible fears. I could not imagine what I had done for God to punish me in this way day in and day out. I believed I was a hideous and horrible person in the eyes of God. Hiding the bad thoughts and the idea of being punished by God from everyone was tormenting. I was living a dual existence. There was the Chrissie everyone else knew, and the Chrissie God knew; the evil Chrissie.

I was exhausted. I hated myself. I hated my life. I wished I could be anyone other than myself.

I barely held it together through the summer with so much time to focus on the obsession without distraction. The constant cycle of doubt made me feel sad and depressed. It seemed endless. I was elated when summer ended and sophomore year began. I needed a busy routine to keep my mind occupied. Not having cheerleading practice would be tough, so I vowed to find another sport to occupy my time. I tried out for every sports team and joined as many clubs as possible.

I was right about having a routine. As soon as I engaged in my busy school life, I felt relief from the pressing stress regarding the obsession. It still lurked in every corner of my mind, but the excitement of school and socializing became more of a focus. Even though I had to continue my rumination, avoidance, prayers, and 'proof' theories, I was relieved to have other things to focus my energy on. I started to feel alive again.

Not long after football season began, I started dating Ryan. I had known him my freshman year, but something felt different this year. We would sit together at football games and he made me laugh constantly. When I was with Ryan, it seemed like the obsession never existed. Our relationship progressed quickly. I was excited about him, but nervous because of all the anxiety and stress I had experienced over the summer. *What if the bad thoughts come back? What if something happens proving I can't be with men once I've gotten into a relationship with him? What if he knew I had these fears last year? What if he thought I didn't really like him and I had to be gay? Doesn't feeling this way about Ryan ultimately 'prove' I like men?*

I had questions saturated in fear as I explored the idea of being with Ryan. But once we crossed the line of being in a relationship, the questions no longer mattered. I was surprised how quickly I fell in love with him. It was so easy and safe with him. I had never experienced a feeling as all-encompassing, vulnerable, and thrilling. This feeling of love overpowered the bad thoughts. I hoped I could consider the thoughts never having any truth after feeling this way about Ryan.

While the thoughts took a backseat to Ryan, they never completely vanished. They popped up in peculiar and annoying ways. Ryan and I would have a blast together, and when he would drop me at home, I would become consumed with bad thoughts and questions. *Maybe you didn't really have a good time? Maybe you are faking having a good time to pretend you aren't supposed to be gay? Maybe you are in denial? If you really aren't supposed to be gay, why would you worry about it in the first place on that night?* These thoughts created surges of panic, but I used my feelings and attraction for Ryan as 'proof' they weren't real. If I wouldn't latch onto the thoughts feeling confident about the 'proof', my brain would tell me because I still worried often meant there must be truth to it. I feared the time I wouldn't be able find enough proof to neutralize the worry. This was my most terrifying and haunting fear.

I stayed committed and focused on the belief I had offended God, therefore I needed to be punished by bad thoughts. When the bad thoughts popped up, I engaged in prayer rituals and days of repentance believing I needed God's forgiveness and mercy. Because the fear had subsided since I met Ryan, it must prove God is pleased with me and my relationship. I was willing to do whatever I could to keep it that way.

As the end of my sophomore year approached, so did my relationship with Ryan. He would be attending college next fall and logically it made sense to break up. However, I could not rationalize this to my heart. I was devastated. My heart was completely shattered. I heard heartbreak was tough, but had no idea it would feel this way. It was like the flu without physical symptoms. The magnitude of losing Ryan was immeasurable. I wasn't sure how I would recover. I wished I could go back to before I met him so I didn't have to feel this horrendous pain. It was overwhelmingly difficult.

But an interesting twist presented itself with the breakup. I found a plus side in the midst of misery. Curled on the floor in a fetal position sobbing uncontrollably, a thought cross my mind:

The fact I am heartbroken obviously proves I do not have to be gay, doesn't it? If I really am not supposed to be with men, I would not have fallen in love with a man, right? And, if I am really not supposed to be with men, I would not be heartbroken over a man, right?

As much as I didn't want to, I felt the need to capture the feeling of being heartbroken in case I needed 'proof' in the future. There was nothing I wanted more than to forget how painful it felt, but I needed to capture and remember it. I could return to this particular moment as 'proof' I did not have to be gay and I really do like men. It was the only positive moment in the months of pain I endured grieving the loss of Ryan.

I could store a memory bank of 'proof theories'. If I was ever attacked by the thoughts again, I could tap into the moments I'd captured to disprove I had to turn gay. I had plenty of them already, and I knew there would be more. My new ritual was to hoard proof. I could arm myself if I were to ever become bombarded with the bad thoughts again. This seemed like a solid plan. I hoped the worst of the bad thoughts were over now, but at least I could hold onto hope if they ever returned. I would be ready to defeat the bad thoughts now with my new 'proof' memory bank.

Chapter 9: If It Is Physical, It Must Be Real?

Summer arrived and I decided the only way to get over the heartbreak was to occupy myself with other guys. The intrusive thoughts diminished significantly once I felt excited about dating. I needed to occupy my mind with excitement instead of being overwhelmed with downtime. Not only was I still hurting from the break up, I feared feeling the depression and misery I experienced last summer. I needed a plan. I had a few little flings that did not involve sex for fear of being punished with the bad thoughts. I believed sex was something God would punish me for, so I stayed clear of it. When I dated guys, it was flirting, kissing, maybe a little making out, but nothing serious. I loved the courtship phase. The bad thoughts disappeared during the phase of elation and excitement over a new guy. But in between crushes, I still felt deep and lingering sadness over the loss of Ryan. I didn't allow myself to grieve and recover from the relationship because I was terrified the bad thoughts would return. The idea of feeling sad and lonely felt like a breeding ground for bad thoughts, so I couldn't allow myself to think about Ryan. I buried the sadness and grief of losing him.

As busy as I tried to keep my days, summer was a dead end with too much empty time. Days progressed without sports and studies, while little spikes of panic popped up frequently and in random places. I was not seeing friends and guys I had crushes on as often, so it was hard to deposit 'proof theories' in my mind. A few weeks into summer, I began losing energy and feeling depressed. I experienced waves of impending doom. During these times, I spent hours alone ruminating, trying to 'prove' or 'disprove' thoughts. As time distanced from school and being with Ryan, I started to believe times the thoughts weren't as bad were never real. *Did I imagine they lessened? Were they bad, but I just pretended they weren't?* It started to feel as if I was slipping away. I began to feel numb.

I sat in my room for days doing nothing but thinking about the bad thoughts, trying to combat them with proof. I was exhausted but couldn't sleep. Sadness and anger about this agony I had endured for so many years weighed on my soul. *Why didn't anyone else go through this?* I ritualistically prayed to God asking forgiveness for whatever I had done to deserve this punishment. I was in agony.

Then out of nowhere, the moods of gloom and doom would break. I would wake up feeling better. The bad thoughts retreated from my mind and I felt relief once more. I believed God had forgiven me for whatever I had done to deserve the thoughts. When the cycle broke, I offered ritualistic prayers of thanks to God. I was so relieved when the cycles ended, yet also paranoid and desperate with worry about if and when the next ones would begin.

When the cycles broke, I became the Chrissie I wanted everyone to know. I became social again, adopting an energetic, encompassing façade for everyone to see. I hoped people wouldn't suspect anything was wrong in between my social times, so when out of a cycle I did everything to be outgoing and over-the-top happy.

I was visiting a relative one weekend, spending most of the day by the neighborhood pool, when I heard the gate slam. I looked up to see a gorgeous, tan, muscular guy walking past me. He caught my eye and butterflies exploded through my chest. I could definitely log him into the 'proof' theory bank! Within an hour, we were in the pool chatting and laughing. I had never felt as sexually attracted to anyone before like I did that day. As I drew closer to him, the movement of water made his boxers flap in front. I saw the outline of a bulge in his shorts. A surge of heat flooded my face, chest, stomach, and then traveled further down. Never before had I experienced a moment of sexual arousal just being in the presence of someone. Terrified he might notice, I backed away a couple of steps. He asked if I was blushing. I replied that I must be getting sunburned. Sinking under the water to cool down, I wanted to look at his shorts again. I opened my eyes, but it was too blurry to see anything. Just the thought of it aroused me again.

I wanted to rip his shorts off right there and have him take me in his arms. I couldn't stop thinking about what he looked like under his shorts. It was erotic, but I knew it was wrong and sinful to feel this way. *God is going to punish me if I keep looking at his shorts.* But, I couldn't stop. I watched every muscle in his tan chest and arms move as he talked and told me stories. All I could think of was how his lips would feel on mine and on my body. I knew I needed to stop thinking about it, but couldn't.

After hanging out all afternoon, he invited me to go out with him and his buddies that evening. I wanted to so badly, but was scared and torn. I was afraid I would be unable to control myself around him and do regrettable things for which I would be punished. I wanted to go because this was singly the best 'proof' I'd ever experienced. Mostly I just wanted to be around him. It was pure chemistry. I wanted to feel aroused by him. I felt exhilarated.

I decided not to go. Fear of being punished was too strong. I hoped God would recognize how I resisted and forgive me for staring at his shorts. All evening I regretted not going with him, but had to focus on staying away from bad thoughts and punishment.

Several weeks later, I still felt butterflies when thinking of him. I wished so badly I had gone out with him. Thinking about him one afternoon, I looked up at the television. A girl with a bathing suit came on the screen. She was muscularly ripped and beautiful. My arousal still lingered about the guy, but then I felt confused. *Why am I still feeling aroused? Did the arousal transfer to the girl when I looked at the television?*

My anxiety intensified. *Who am I aroused by, my guy in the pool or this girl on the television? No, I was thinking about the guy first and then looked at the girl! Or was I just thinking about the guy, then saw the girl and then felt aroused? Oh my God, did I get aroused by the girl? Am I aroused now?*

I searched every corner of my mind for answers on whether or not I was aroused, why I was aroused, and by whom. I couldn't look at the TV again. *What if I looked at the TV and the girl came on and I got aroused and that proved I was really aroused by her and not the guy with the shorts and it proves I have to be gay?* I needed to see. I needed 'proof'. I peeked at the television with one eye closed. A lady appeared on the screen and I began worrying. *Do I think she is attractive? Did I just get aroused?* I searched my sensations down there to figure out if I had become aroused or if it was just left-over from when I was thinking about the guy in the pool. *Am I aroused at this random lady on the television commercial? I think I felt something down there. Did something move? Was it really arousal or was it left over from me thinking about the guy? Or was it left over from me seeing the girl because she aroused me and I only thought the guy did? OH MY GOD!*

The 'arousal reaction' became part of the bad thoughts every day. I would see a cute guy and analyze if I felt aroused. I would see a pretty girl and analyze if I felt aroused. If I sensed something moving down there, I saw it as ultimate 'proof' or 'disproof'. But, I felt it all the time. It accompanied anything and everything associated with the bad thoughts. There was a distinct difference between what happened in the pool with the guy and his shorts and this new 'arousal reaction', but I couldn't figure out a way to put it to rest. Just like the bad thoughts, when the arousal with the bad thoughts happened I experienced the bad feelings of not being able to breathe, tingling in my neck and arms, and an overwhelming sense of needing to escape.

I believed this feeling in my groin was punishment from God. I knew in the pool what I was doing and feeling was wrong in His eyes. I should have left the pool. Now because I took pleasure in looking at the guy in the pool, I would be punished with this heinous sensation. I prayed for forgiveness, but found no relief. This arousal reaction was going to keep me trapped. There was no way to find out how or why it was happening, so I'd never be able to escape the doubt. This must be God's ultimate and direct punishment for sinning in the pool. I wished I had never met that guy. I wished I had not gone to the pool that day. I wished to be anyone else because living my life was miserable.

I sank into a deep cycle of rumination and depression after the development of the arousal reaction. I felt dirty and disgusting. I felt guilty for the horrible physical feelings. I didn't want them, but they wouldn't stop. Everyone I looked at caused the feeling and I couldn't make it stop. I loathed myself. I was the worst person on earth. Rationally I knew the thoughts and arousal feelings weren't real, but being unable to make them stop made me feel weak and stupid. Because those mental and physical feelings weren't something I wanted or desired, I felt embarrassed and ashamed. *What kind of person thinks about these things for hours and hours trying to find proof either way? But, don't physical feelings prove these thoughts are real? Didn't I feel real arousal in the pool with the guy? Why wouldn't that be enough proof to stop all of the arousal tests I have to have every day?*

I also felt ashamed because I did not believe being gay was wrong or bad. Having anxiety toward the thoughts and feelings made me feel hypocritical. *Did this mean I hated gay people? I did not hate homosexuals at all, so why were the thoughts so appalling to me if I didn't feel that way about gay people?* The entire scenario was confusing and exhausting. I didn't believe gay people were bad, but I didn't believe I was or wanted to be gay. I couldn't understand why knowing these facts wasn't enough to convince me. *What kind of idiot was I not to trust my own thoughts?*

As soon as I convinced myself the gay fear was unwarranted, I was thrown into secondary fear paralyzing all of my theories. *If I really knew I wasn't supposed to be gay, I wouldn't worry about whether I actually was all of this time and I wouldn't have physical reactions, right?* The constant questioning and cycling for hours upon hours, day after day, wore me down. Every night I prayed to God for mercy, hoping to awaken with relief. It tore down my self-esteem. It wore on my ability to foresee any sort of future for myself. I was rotting on the inside. While it seemed everyone around me was blessed with a 'normal' brain, I endured this intense torture at the hands of a God who was supposed to love and protect me. I felt completely alone. I wanted to tell someone, but if I did, wouldn't it be proof the thoughts were real? I was the loneliest human being on the planet.

Junior year was rapidly approaching and despite the overpowering sadness weighing on my mind, I made a snap decision of empowerment. I decided with nothing to lose, I had to take a risk. I was sick of waking up every day fearful of the bad thoughts. I was tired of worrying all the time whether or not I had done something to offend God. I would become part of every possible school club, team, and activity to avoid dealing with this crap by keeping myself busy. This summer had proved my time on earth was limited. I couldn't maintain this façade much longer now that it had triggered a physical response. It was only a matter of time before misery overtook me and I would have to complete suicide. I needed to do whatever I could to enjoy the time I had before then. No matter what, I would do everything I could to stave off the miserable cycles and suicide by being as busy as humanly possible.

School starts in one week. I have a plan and I feel liberated. I have to be stronger than the thoughts. I have to do everything I can to block them out. I have to find a way to be a good enough person so the thoughts will leave me alone. I want to believe this. I want to believe I am strong enough. I want to believe I deserve this last chance.

Deep down I knew I was lying to myself. One day this thing in my mind would bring me to my knees. It would bring me to the end. I wouldn't be able to escape death by my own hands. Believing I could control it was an illusion. I knew this at my core, but needed to somehow believe there was more time before the end.

For now, I have to take advantage of life. I don't know how much time I have left, and I want to soak up every moment I can. I will enjoy every moment I am granted relief by my brain and by God, until they turn on me again. When it is time to die, I will honor that. But for now, I need to live while I still have the chance.

Chapter 10: Trapped By a Monster

Junior year began with a vengeance. I joined every club possible, dove into my studies, and was more social than ever. I wanted to meet anyone who would talk to me. Knowing life would end soon, I felt immune to frivolous social hierarchies. I wondered if anyone else suffered in silence the way I did. I wanted to find connections with other humans in hopes of not feeling so alone. I didn't care who was the most popular, smartest, or least accepted socially. I only wanted to enjoy people for who they were. I believed if I saw past other's outside, maybe someone would accept me despite who I was on the inside. Also, I did everything I could to stay busy in an effort to ward off the bad thoughts.

And then, there was Jared.

I had known Jared casually since freshman year, but we had never spent time together. Our paths crossed beginning of junior year and we quickly found there was more than an attraction between us. He was funny, clever, and our chemistry was invigorating. I fell head over heels in love with him. Just like clockwork, as soon as I began my relationship with Jared, the bad thoughts took a backseat. It was a relief they calmed down since the summer had been so intense. I hoped with my decision to stay busy and now being with Jared, the bad thoughts would disappear for good. Or at the least I hoped they would be comparable to my throw up worries, appearing every so often but easily manageable.

Our relationship progressed and we became serious for the next year-and-a-half. The bad thoughts were always there just as the throw up thoughts were, but with less frequency as the summer after my freshman and sophomore years. Despite not being present every moment, when they did appear they were just as paralyzing and tormenting as ever. I noticed the bad thoughts and feelings would appear during stress and/or downtime. Holidays were hard because they lacked routine. Finals and stressful basketball games or track meets caused the thoughts to flare up. Also, whenever I had fights or drama with Jared or friends, the thoughts overtook me. I dreaded relationship/friendship dramas because I knew my brain would default to latching onto the bad thoughts.

Typical panic spikes threw me into longer cycles. Fear-mongering TV shows like 20/20 or 60 Minutes about being gay or turning gay caused panic. I worried the shows were some kind of 'sign' I was supposed to be gay. When I met women I thought were pretty, I ruminated on whether I thought they were pretty because I just thought they were pretty or did that 'prove' that I was attracted to them. When I saw men thinking they were good-looking, I worried I really didn't think they were and maybe I was pretending in order to disprove the theory of the bad thoughts. When I heard 'anti-gay' propaganda I wondered if God was reminding me to be a good person or He would punish me with the bad thoughts. I constantly sought forgiveness for anything I believed could offend Him. I tried to be the best Christian I could to stay in His good graces. My life revolved around making sure God was happy with me in order to avoid punishment.

When the bad thoughts and feelings abated, other tortuous feelings became prevalent. I constantly battled feelings of hopelessness and worthlessness. I was acutely aware of being a phony to the outside world regarding my fears and anxieties. I did my best to portray a social, Christian, outgoing, happy, and successful girl. In reality, I was a frightened, empty, shameful, and guilt-ridden girl unable to control or manage her thoughts. I felt guilty. I felt weak and stupid. My self-esteem was next to nothing. I believed I was the lowest common denominator of a human being. I was the scum of the earth.

Self-sabotage was a destructive factor through good and bad times. It haunted me as much as the bad thoughts. I believed no matter how good things became, there would always be a crash. There would inevitably be a time to face everything and possibly take my own life. I was on borrowed time. Anything good in my life was an illusion, because I did not deserve anything good. I was unworthy of a happy and good life. Anytime I challenged these internal beliefs, my brain would remind me how long I had been suffering and punished by God. Naturally, I would fall back into the self-deprecating cycle.

I constantly wondered if everyone knew how easy they had it. I couldn't believe how petty and frivolous people's worries were sometimes. My friends became worked up over the stupidest things, and I wondered how nice it would be to only worry about those little things. Did they have any clue how bad it could be? I also wondered if there were others like me, too afraid to say it out loud. I longed to tell someone everything I had been through. I wanted to hear someone say it was okay and I was not a horrible person. I also wondered if merely saying it out loud might release some of the anxiety. Just getting this secret I had been carrying all these years off my chest seemed desirable. But, I knew it was not an option.

No one would say I was not a horrible person if they knew the truth, because they would see that I was. No one would understand. And even more frightening, no one would believe me. They would just believe I was crazy for worrying about throwing up and being in the closet. I knew something wasn't right. I knew the thoughts weren't real. I knew there had to be a logical explanation, but what could it be? There was no simple or rational explanation. I had the thoughts for too long not to believe there was some truth behind them.

How could my thoughts and reactions be anything but real? How could they be wrong, right? Wouldn't I be able to know if what I thought and felt wasn't right or correct based on how I interpreted, responded, and perceived the world around me? It doesn't make sense for the bad thoughts to be right, but it doesn't make sense for them to be wrong either.

I felt deep sadness that no one really knew me, only the persona I created. They only knew the person I wanted them to think they knew. What would everyone think if they knew all the things that went on in my head? What would they do if they knew every day of my life I had to be vigilant in controlling my environment out of fear? Would they still like me? Would they be disappointed in me? Would they judge me? Would they reject me?

I felt alone most of the time. Outwardly, I was a giant personality of light and happiness. On the inside I was dark, sad, and terrified. My existence consisted of pleasing God and making sure every move projected the correct image to hide the truth. The more people I could convince nothing was wrong, the more I felt in control, at least to the outside world. But unfortunately, I knew this control was an illusion. I was keenly aware of having lost control of my mind many years ago when I was eight years old. And the idea I had suffered for so many years in silence gave my brain more fuel to convince me that if I am still suffering, there must be truth behind all of it, keeping me trapped in the cycle.

The world saw me as having it all together. But I was trapped by a monster. I was alone and terrified every single day. I was losing the battle, and no amount of façade to the outside world covered that up.

Chapter 11: College: A Reprieve

I graduated from Osborne High School in 1995. I was proud and surprised to have made it without completing suicide. My senior year was occupied being with Jared and busy submitting college applications. Although I regularly battled hopelessness and bad thoughts, the high school environment I had been in for four years was familiar, safe, and comfortable. College seemed foreign and scary. I had managed to convince my high school peers I was not the horrible person I believed myself to be. How could I start over in an unfamiliar environment? What if they saw through me? What if I entered an unbreakable cycle of bad thoughts and feelings? What if things became bad like they did the summer after sophomore year? The 'what if' questions were endless and tormenting.

My relationship with Jared ended as quickly as senior year finished. We were going to separate schools and the best decision was to part ways. I felt the familiar sting of heartbreak. I was sad and devastated. Again, I felt as if I were sick with a symptomless flu almost the entire summer. It was agonizing. I remembered how difficult things became the summer after losing Ryan and I felt scared. *What if things get really bad before I leave for college? How can I begin college in a miserable cycle of bad thoughts?* I needed to stay busy, so I started a regimen of running daily and working as a cashier at Publix grocery store.

I was also able to log the sad feelings and heartbreak experience into the 'proof theory' bank. My last two years being with Jared seemed enough to 'prove' anything. I had been so in love with him, but I knew my brain didn't work rationally. I never knew when I would need to remember my life didn't always reflect the bad thoughts. It was bittersweet. However, I would have chosen to have Jared back any day over the proof theory of memories. I was so immersed in sadness.

Despite the heartbreak, I recommitted to the pledge I made before junior year to stave off the bad thoughts. I would tuck the heartbreak away and deal with it later if needed. I decided to be as busy, social, and successful as possible at college. I entered Georgia Southern University with enthusiasm and excitement. My first year of college, I truly believed the bad thoughts might be gone forever. I rarely experienced anxiety and when the bad thoughts arose, I told my mind I was too busy to acknowledge them. I shrugged them off and thought about all the new people and fun things I was experiencing. To my surprise, my mindset was effective.

Everywhere at college there was someone new to meet, something new to experience, and somewhere new to go. I loved living on my own and having independence. I rushed Alpha Delta Pi sorority and made so many friends. I soaked up every experience and attended every event I could to stay busy and occupied. I decided to believe the bad thoughts were merely a phase and a thing of the past.

However, I made sure to keep my Christian outlook, maintaining a life as virtually sin-free as possible, just in case. Even though the bad thoughts seemed buried, I cautiously reminded myself about the possibility of waking up to be haunted by them again. I figured with the temptations of college, God must be very proud of me for staying strong because He had not plagued my mind with bad thoughts since I started. Every once in a while I experienced a twinge of panic, but would be vigilant in my prayer rituals and ruminations for a couple of days. I assumed I made a minor mistake and needed God's forgiveness or maybe He was testing me. But overall, I felt God was proud of me for being a good enough person and Christian and didn't feel the need to punish me.

My freshman year flew by, and it was a blast. I never felt as alive as I did that year. I soaked up every moment as a reprieve from the hell I had experienced for so many years. In late spring, I was recruited to the Georgia Southern Cross-Country team for the following year. I was elated and overwhelmed with excitement. I would be returning my sophomore year to live with my friends in the sorority house as a collegiate athlete. God must be proud of the person I was now. He was rewarding me with these great things and didn't need to punish me so often. I felt so grateful for His mercy. Perhaps those years of torment were a test to see how faithful I would be to Him. Perhaps I had proven I was a true Christian and He would no longer need to inflict bad thoughts and punishment on me.

To solidify my commitment to God, I became a summer camp counselor at Camp Glisson, a Christian summer camp in the North Georgia mountains. This haven was a coveted escape. Camp was filled with college kids as counselors and all ages of kids as campers. This felt like the culmination of my spiritual journey. I believed everything I had been through the past ten years washed away in eight short summer weeks. I dealt with the throw up fear often throughout the summer, but I believed I handled it easily with faith and God's help through prayer rituals and avoidance. Kids would get sick, overheated, and homesick, drumming up fears of being contaminated and exposed. I remained diligent with rituals and prayers hoping God would show His pride in the person I had become. I believed I was handling the throwing up anxiety much better than before. I saw it as a sign the debilitating cycles might never happen again.

Of course, summer camp brought summer romance. The long summer days and common spiritual interests made camp a breeding ground for high intensity romance. I loved these all-encompassing relationships and they contradicted everything I worried about with the gay bad thoughts. How could I be so smitten and engulfed in lust by these summer flings if I was really supposed to turn gay? These summers seemed to be the ultimate 'proof' I needed. It solidified me because I was in line with worshiping God. He removed the thoughts and allowed me to have these intense and incredible relationships. It was the definitive proof that as long as I was right with God, I would never be overtaken by the thoughts. Everything seemed so easy now.

Until it wasn't.

Chapter 12: The Beginning of the End

The summer ended, and leaving Camp Glisson felt like a heartbreak. I had lived in a dream world for two months, and felt ripped apart leaving. While I loved college, I was going back to a stressful class schedule and a full-time cross-country training schedule. I had never run cross-country, and didn't have a clue how intense and stringent college athletics would be. I felt nervous about balancing a sorority, studying, and my first cross-country season. I needed to lean on God for help and support to make sure the bad thoughts didn't come back. I would neither have the time nor energy to battle them this year.

My classes and cross-country training schedule were grueling and exhausting. I was tired every day. I underestimated how toiling the physical demands of cross-country would be on my body. While other members of the team had been running for years, I had only run as a pastime. My body was not used to two running sessions per day, speed workouts on the track, and weight lifting on top of it. It pushed my body beyond an athletic capacity I ever knew I had. It was excruciatingly exhausting.

The throw up obsession presented itself often at the sorority house. Sorority girls are partiers. It was not uncommon to walk into a bathroom late at night and hear someone throwing up or see someone passed out on the bathroom floor by the toilet. Logically, I could reconcile it was due to alcohol, but still needed to ask appropriate questions to ensure I had proof I wouldn't catch anything. I spent many nights worrying who was getting sick and how I could find out why they were sick.

Throwing up was also common in cross-country. People become overheated and sick after running and I would have to see and hear it. No one else flinched. I always needed to find out why people were sick even though it seemed logical it was from overheating or exhaustion. I was concerned how overbearing the throw up fears were becoming. *What am I doing to deserve this? Why is God letting this happen around me? I haven't changed how I'm living, so why is God mad at me?*

Toward the end of cross-country season, I met a football player named Jacob. He had strawberry-blonde hair and the straightest, whitest teeth I had ever seen. Several inches taller than me, he had an incredible body and infectious smile. I felt so lanky and dorky in my running shorts and sports bra, covered head to toe in sweat and salt, when I first saw him. But when he walked past me, looked me straight in the eye and said "Hello", I almost melted into the pavement. I muttered something back that I hoped sounded coherent. Each day after our first encounter, I made sure I was in the same spot at the same time so I could see him again. Over the next several weeks, we figured out a way to talk and eventually he asked me on a date.

An incredible athlete, he was straight-laced, didn't drink, smoke, or cuss, and was very religious. This was perfect so I could stay on a straight and narrow path for God. He respected my views on religion and sex. I was not going to even venture down the sex road despite our incredible attraction to each other. I avoided the bad thoughts for such a long stretch and wasn't about to risk it on anyone. He was okay with it. However it was difficult, because making out with him was the most intense I had experienced. I had never felt as sexually attracted to anyone I dated before as I did to him. We had undeniable chemistry. His body was chiseled and gorgeous. It was hard to be vigilant in my beliefs with him. But I weighed the options of having the bad thoughts versus resisting sex, and there was no question in my mind which to choose. I believed my temptation with Jacob was a test from God and wanted to use it as a way to prove to God how good of a Christian woman I could be. Maybe God would see my dedication and take the thoughts away for good.

Late spring, Jacob, several friends, and I went to 'The Rocking Horse' dance club on a Thursday evening. Afterward, Jacob walked me to the door and before I could reach for the handle, the door swung open unexpectedly. Jessica, a girl in my sorority, had been waiting for me to return. I walked inside and the kitchen light indicated the urgency that something wasn't right.

"Chrissie, you need to call your mother. She said it doesn't matter what time you get home. It is an emergency."

The urgency in her voice was palpable. I looked at Jacob, frozen with fear. I felt paralyzed. I couldn't move, but wanted to run. What if something had happened to my sister or my dad? I didn't want to call. I didn't want to hear what had happened. I stood still, searching Jessica's face for answers, but she had no more information to give me.

Jacob picked up the phone and handed it to me. My hands shook as I slowly dialed the number. I hesitated to finish dialing, but took a breath, closed my eyes and pressed the last number.

The phone barely rang on the other end before mama picked up.

"Hello?"

"It's me. I'm sorry it is so late, but we were out tonight. Is...is something wrong?"

"It's your cousin, John."

My heart sank.

"What. What? What about John?"

"He's missing."

"Missing. Missing? What does that mean? What does missing mean?"

"He went missing off the coast of Texas in a sailboat. He was with friends. They got stranded on an island and now they cannot find him."

"Um…it's JOHN!? The most intelligent, most capable, most incredible person I know. He is fine. He is probably with friends partying or something. What is the big deal? Why is everyone panicking? It's JOHN. He is fine. This is a joke, right?"

"No, Chrissie. They have been searching for a long time. They don't think they will find him."

"This is ridiculous. I have to go."

"I need you to drive to grandma's house in Macon tomorrow and meet us. Joy will be there. Can you find a way to get there? I am leaving tomorrow and I need you to be there."

"No. I can't think about this. NO. I have to go."

I slammed my hand on the phone to hang up before mama could respond. I backed into the wall sliding down to the floor with the phone still in my hand. *Not my John. My beloved, cherished cousin and friend. My cousin like my brother. My brother like my best friend. There is no way in this world anything would happen to him. He is the smartest, most genuine, most incredible person I know. He is probably off somewhere just fooling around with friends. This is wrong. There is no way something has happened to him.*

My eyes glazed over. I felt numb. I couldn't hear anything. I felt as if I were rising out of my body toward the ceiling. I didn't want to be in that kitchen anymore. I wanted to run, but I couldn't move. I couldn't speak. I wanted to jump up and tear out of the house and the town. But, I was paralyzed. *Where was John? Where was he? Is this real? This cannot be real life?*

I felt a hand on my shoulder and then my neck. Jacob sat directly in front of me asking what he could do to help.

"Nothing. I want to be alone. I need to be alone. I can't talk. I need to be alone."

He hugged me and asked what had happened. I stared blankly at him. I couldn't speak. I said John's name, then told him I needed to be alone. He said his goodbyes and left. I was glad. I didn't want to talk to anyone.

A black hole of darkness pierced my chest at the thought of losing one of my best friends. John was a rare soul-mate who understood and loved me without question, concern, or second thought. He was quiet and reserved. I was bold and vibrant. We saw qualities in each other we sought for ourselves but couldn't quite master. Our difference in personality made us match so perfectly in harmonious friendship. We spent time together over high school summers exploring, talking about relationships, dreams, and goals on vacations with my dad at the Big Canoe resort. I brought friends and he would fall in love with them. I giggled at his innocence and lack of 'game' playing, while he would pine over how much he liked them. We stayed up nights playing stupid card games or Nintendo, laughing at the most ridiculous things. We had stupid inside-jokes that didn't even make sense to us. We could be silent together or we could run screaming across the golf course through the sprinklers. We watched stupid movies together and memorized quotes to laugh at over and over. I was free to be my stupid, dorky self with him without judgment. He could be whoever he wanted around me knowing I would adore him anyway. It was one of the most authentic relationships I ever had.

There were moments during our summer adventures I thought about opening up to him about my bad thoughts. If there was anyone in the world who would love and accept me despite the bad, I knew it would be John. Several times, I started to tell him. In the midst of the horrible times, I always wanted to call him. But, fear kept me silent. The 'what if's' stopped me. I believed if I told him and lost his trust and love, I would never forgive myself. During the most difficult times with my illness through the years, I longed for the times I spent with John. Our respect and adoration for one another was a rare escape. Our good times were a refuge for me and a reminder of goodness and hope in the world. He taught me the meaning of unconditional love and acceptance.

I could barely comprehend the magnitude of the impact losing John would have on me. I swear I could hear the sound of my heart crack open as I rolled into a fetal position on the kitchen floor. Tears spilled sideways, dripping onto the cold tile. I wanted to run away. I wished I could go back to only a few hours ago before I knew any of this. *Maybe he is really okay? Maybe he is just lost?*

There was no way to prove or disprove my way out of this. I couldn't use avoidance or reassurance to escape this pain. How was I going to face this? How could I ever accept and recover from this? Deep down, I knew the truth. I heard it in mama's voice. He was gone, and in that moment I knew a large part of myself drifted away with him. The only good inside of me went with him. I felt a dark void in my chest, and I could sense the danger in the darkness. There was no way out of this, and I knew it. Instinctively, I knew this was the beginning of the end for me.

Chapter 13: Small Cracks in a Hardened Shell

Jessica tried to force me off the floor, but I couldn't move. I was paralyzed with sadness and fear. *What do I do now? How can I keep living?* I could think of no one else to call but Brad, one of my best friends. We dated on and off the last year and a half, but could not make it work. Regardless, my affection and trust for him exceeded everyone I knew at Georgia Southern. I knew how much Brad cared about me, and I needed to be with someone I loved and someone who loved me.

It was 2:30am when Brad's roommate answered the phone. He refused to call Brad. I was screaming and threatening him by the time he reluctantly agreed. I was hoping and praying Brad would accept my call when I heard his voice pierce the silence. I sobbed the words of John's disappearance between heaving breaths. Almost as quickly as I blinked my eyes, Brad was banging on the back door. Brad knew the depth of love and admiration I had for John. He often teased me about no man being able to live up to the relationship I had with John.

Brad comforted me in every capacity as I became lost in grief. He made sure I was safe. He held me. He listened to me scream and cry. He sat patiently in silence with me. He did not leave my side. He grieved *with me* for someone he didn't know. He held me together as I fell apart. I do not know what I would have done without him.

After only an hour or so of sleep, I woke up to a full day of classes and a shattered heart. I hoped it had been a dream, but when I saw Brad on the couch, I knew it really happened. I held onto hope the phone would ring any moment confirming John was safe. Every minute ticked by as if waiting on my own execution. I went to my first class and put my head down on the desk, silently crying onto my text book. I didn't want anyone to know I was upset. It was hard to listen to everyone chatting and laughing like nothing was wrong. I didn't want to be there. I felt I was going to panic, like the bad thoughts caused me to do. My head started feeling hot. I looked around for an escape when I locked eyes with Brad's roommate. I wondered if he hated me after I yelled at him last night. He walked over and put his hand on mine. I apologized for yelling at him. He told me how sorry he was for my loss. I looked up at him as the tears rolled down my face. At least one person in this room knew what had happened, so I didn't feel as alone.

Brad was waiting outside my class to take me to my favorite restaurant for lunch. I ordered my favorite salad. It had slices of cheddar cheese cut like those cartoon mice ate. They were always in a perfect triangle which somehow made the salad so much better. Today, I just moved the cheese and salad around on my plate with the fork. The lump in my throat kept me from eating. Brad was talking to me, but I couldn't hear anything he was saying. I was going through the motions, but felt like I had disappeared somewhere. Brad said my name out loud. I looked at him. He slid his car keys over to me telling me to drive to Macon to see my family. I snapped into reality.

I didn't want to go. I wanted to stay. I wanted everything to be the same as it was before yesterday. If I went to Macon, this would be real. I wanted to stay and pretend everything was okay and John was still alive.

Brad looked at me like he knew the questions I was contemplating. He said I needed to go and find out the truth. He reassured me I would return by Sunday because he needed his car Monday morning. This made me feel better. I hung onto his words. I needed to believe I would return and everything would return to normal. So, I agreed. I packed a small bag and headed to Macon, Georgia, to see my mom, grandmother, and sister. I tried to believe I would receive good news upon arrival.

Friday night and Saturday came and went with no news. I pretended to study in an effort to avoid everyone, but could not concentrate on anything but my swirling thoughts. I knew having no news was not good. I wished I had never left Statesboro. I hated being trapped with my family in this uncertainty. I needed distraction. Without a routine I knew the bad thoughts would start to simmer, especially with this crisis. I couldn't feel them yet, but I knew the situation was not good. I felt a deep uneasiness and it was frightening.

Mama talking on the phone woke me early Sunday morning. I was on the horribly uncomfortable sofa bed facing the wooden paneling on my grandma's living room walls. The tone of her voice confirmed what I already knew. I feigned asleep to avoid facing her. She told grandma they had found John. He was dead. He had drowned.

I closed my eyes, fighting back tears. I didn't want to cry in front of anyone. I wanted to be alone. I wanted to get into Brad's car and drive away. I didn't want to comfort anyone or be comforted. I needed to feel numb. I didn't want to feel any of this. I didn't think I could handle letting one ounce of this pain hit my heart. I would fall apart, and I wasn't prepared to see what that looked like.

I felt mama's hand on my shoulder. Without looking at her, I told her I was awake and heard the update. I never looked at her or anyone else. Like a robot, I got out of bed and packed my things. I showered and got dressed. I refused to engage in sadness and grieving in that moment. I packed Brad's car and told my family I needed to go back to school. Mama was yelling at me to stay. I did not care. I needed to get out of that house and be alone. I needed to get away from the news and grief.

I pointed the car south on I-75 toward Statesboro. The road was clear ahead of me. I floored the gas to over 100mph, gripping the steering wheel so tightly my knuckles ached. At the time, I did not even realize I was screaming with tears streaming down my face. I did not care if I crashed or if the car blew up. My heart was on fire. It felt like my insides were being ripped apart. My John was gone. I would never see him again. I would never hear his laugh again. I would never see his face again. We would never tell our stupid inside jokes again. I felt dissociated from my body and mind. I didn't care if I lived or died.

When I pulled into the parking space, Brad was racing out his door before I could shut off the engine. He grabbed me as soon as my feet hit the pavement. I think he knew John had passed when I first told him he was missing. I believe he held hope and optimism to support and protect me, all the while knowing the truth. He walked me to the passenger side of his car, shutting the door behind me. We drove back roads for the next three hours. I let the wind blow through my hair from the passenger window. I cried, I closed my eyes, I lay in a fetal position, I spoke out loud to John, I screamed, I held my head out of the window, I laughed, and I sobbed. Brad never said a word. He just drove and let me be what I needed to be. It was the most incredible act of love and support anyone could have given me.

Brad is a great man.

As we pulled into the driveway of the sorority house, I saw mama's car in the parking lot. I panicked. She told me we were driving to Texas for the funeral. I couldn't face it. I couldn't do that. I yelled, cried, and screamed. I resisted and protested. I begged to stay at school. I begged to not go. But in the end, there was no way out. I knew I had to go. I knew I had to at least show my face at the funeral.

We drove almost twenty hours to and from Texas with several days in between the trip there and back. I can barely recall any memories from that trip. Snippets of memory on the night we arrived and moments at the funeral stand out. But, the pain was too intense to be present. I had to be numb to make it through. It was a loss that cut so deep, I wasn't sure I ever wanted to feel again. My mind refused to allow me to feel the trauma of the trip, and I was grateful to be numb and protected from reality. However the repression of emotion and pain would come back and haunt me.

On returning to Georgia Southern, I pretended nothing had happened. I buried the grief. A thick layer of denial hardened around the black hole in my heart. I didn't want to experience the pain associated with losing John, so I did everything possible not to face it. I reasoned as long as I didn't acknowledge it, it would not affect me.

But, the small cracks in the hardened shell were enough to allow the darkness to slowly seep through. I never recovered from the deep rooted anger and sadness I tucked away from the loss. My fake persona was no longer enough to sustain me. My eyes permanently glazed over with disdain and emptiness. The sunlight in my spirit was setting, and the cold dark night began to permeate my soul. I had been balancing on a tight rope for years, juggling a powerful, unknown illness, and losing one of my best friends began unraveling the rope underneath me. I was getting ready to fall fast into a dark hole hoping for a soft place to land, but knowing the bottom would smash me into a thousand pieces.

It was only a matter of time.

Chapter 14: Is It Time to Die?

After John died, I pretended everything was fine for the duration of spring semester. If I could just hang on until my safe haven as a counselor at Camp Glisson, I believed I would be okay. Being at camp would take away the trauma and pain. I could lose myself in camp's healing power. I was an incredible actor when needing to cover up stress and negative emotions, so camp was the perfect place to buy time and heal. No one would ever have to know the deep distress I was burying. I just needed to make it until then.

I was relieved to see familiar faces from the previous summer when I arrived at camp. I could breathe and safely let go knowing I would be spending the summer in the beautiful mountains. I could take this time to solidify my relationship with God. I had begun to experience some of the bad thoughts at the end of the year under pressure of finals. It scared me, but I held onto hope by anticipating summer camp.

Things started the same way as they had the year before. I met so many people with lively and infectious energy. I immediately fell into a summer romance with Steve. We were acquaintances last summer, but this year we got to know each other and quickly clicked. The first few weeks were relieving and all-encompassing, and took my mind off the trauma of losing John.

But something felt different this year. There was an underlying numbness. I couldn't shake the deep darkness inside. I didn't want to touch it or face it. I was scared of it. I couldn't deny my symptoms of grief much longer and they began to manifest uncontrollably. I felt angry he was gone. I couldn't contain my sadness. I just wanted to be over his death already. If I looked at the reality of his passing straight in the face, I might never recover. I was more content in denial. Even more frightening was how angry I felt at God. Why would He take my beloved cousin? I couldn't come to terms feeling angry with Him. I knew I couldn't be angry with God or He'd punish me. I felt I was betraying Him. But I couldn't stop the feelings of pain and anger toward God over losing John. I was afraid I was intentionally opening myself up for punishment, but couldn't stop those powerful emotions.

After a few weeks, I felt the magic of my summer hideaway being stolen by grief and it angered me. By summer's end, I felt like an outsider. No one treated me differently, but the darkness inside was spreading beyond a space I could contain. I was such a master at masking my feelings, it was almost terrifying. No one suspected the simmering negativity I kept at bay. Everyone saw the happy, energetic, and faithful Chrissie they always knew. It baffled me how convincing my deceit could be.

The thought of leaving Camp Glisson with uncertainty was frightening. *What if I was not able to solidify my relationship with God while I was here? What if God was angry about my anger toward Him at losing John? What if my focus on grief instead of worship made God mad?* When school began, I would be swept in a flurry of cross-country, studies, and sorority. There would be no time to make up to God what I possibly missed at camp. I felt guilty. I felt nervous. I felt out of control.

I drove away from camp toward college with a heavy heart, full of fear. I committed to staying in touch with Steve during the school year. If I held onto him, maybe I could recall the serenity and safety of camp if I needed 'proof' against the bad thoughts. Steve's college was far from Georgia Southern. I knew it would be difficult to try a long distance relationship, but I needed something solid to hold onto. I needed hope.

I was coming back to a convoluted relationship with Jacob, who I left hanging by a string upon my departure when I left last semester. My commitment to Steve faded somewhere between Atlanta and Statesboro. I believed we could stay in touch, but realized how unrealistic it was to try to make it work. I felt devastated. My head pounded as I turned into the driveway of the sorority house. My friends were excited to be living in the house, but I couldn't care less. My energy was depleted. Why was it so exhausting to feel and act excited? It felt like chains shackled my feet as I exited the car and began walking toward the front porch. I heard how fake my voice sounded as I greeted everyone. I saw how fake my actions were as I hugged and pretended to be excited. Something was different now. It was bad. I was fading away from wanting and caring about convincing everyone I was okay. I was becoming indifferent. I felt I should panic, but didn't have the energy to fuel it. I couldn't figure it out in my head, so I just pretended to be the Chrissie everyone expected. I tried to be the Chrissie I wished I could really be.

The whirlwind of back to school activities began the moment I put my suitcase down. There were parties, sorority events, cross-country practices, and a new semester of challenging classes. Apparently fall semester was in full swing, but I just stood still watching it swirl around me like a tornado. My system was shutting down. I carefully exerted enough energy to maintain the appearance everything was great, but I was keenly aware of being in danger of collapsing at any moment.

I couldn't concentrate and stopped caring about anything halfway through the semester. Every ounce of energy was mustered to keep up an image of enthusiasm for my cross-country team. Fall semester is racing season and my performance that year was horrible. Running was my refuge and while I wanted to care and do well, I could not find solace or peace in my feet hitting the pavement. The overpowering depression and sadness was sucking anything I once considered joyous out of my life. It was discouraging. It was lonely. I needed help and was too afraid to ask.

The bad thoughts and feelings were all-consuming. I wasn't surprised. I knew I had let God down at camp by being so preoccupied with grief. The wrath of His punishment was more than I had ever felt before, and I had no fight inside to try to make it better. It was tragic. I knew which rituals to do to stay on top of the thoughts, but I was too tired. There was no point anymore. No matter what I did, the thoughts always returned. They never left. I could never be good enough in God's eyes to be rid of them for good. What was the point in trying to fight them anymore? While the bad thoughts and feelings previously came and went in waves, now the impact felt like a tsunami. It was constant and overwhelming, and I simply didn't have the energy or drive to fight anymore.

I used my chemistry with Jacob as a tool for 'proof' and 'disproof'. I wasn't interested in him or anyone, but needed someone or something to use as a compulsion. We weren't compatible except in our attraction for each other, so it only seemed logical to use it as an advantage until this horrible phase passed. My brain had a field day reasoning this way. It cycled around why I wouldn't want to be in a relationship with him if I truly believed he was hot? Rationally, I knew he wasn't my type, but rationality didn't matter in my downtrodden state of mind.

Once my brain latched onto worrying about not liking him, fires needing to be extinguished popped up everywhere. Each place I looked, my brain spun questions about who and what I was and wasn't attracted to. I could look at a dog and worry if I were sexually attracted to it or not. The more I fought the bad thoughts, the worse they became. The arousal feelings were present twenty-four-seven about anyone and everyone which made things even worse. I could look at men or women and worry whether or not I felt aroused. It was all blending together now. I couldn't go anywhere or look at anyone without my head spinning with questions. I wanted to stay away from everyone. I wanted to disappear.

I tried normal tactics recalling feelings to 'prove' I was not supposed to be gay, but I didn't have the energy to fight the way I did before. My mind told me maybe I faked those feelings before and really didn't feel them. It was brutal. There seemed to be no way out this time. I prayed for peace. I begged for mercy because I sensed time was running out. I was pummeled with bad thoughts day in and day out. I never before experienced them with such magnitude and intensity the way I experienced them now.

Avoidance became my primary compulsion and escape. I avoided places and people on campus I associated with bad thoughts or physical arousal reactions. If I sat on a bench and experienced anxiety or panic, I would leave the bench and intentionally avoid the bench moving forward. Just thinking about the bench would cause anxiety, thus the bench became an avoidance compulsion. Many anxiety triggers made no logical sense and I wanted to challenge their validity, but I couldn't argue with the arousal reactions. Even if the anxiety seemed ridiculous, if it was accompanied by an arousal reaction, there was nothing I could do to 'disprove' the reality.

Every move was controlled by anxiety. I avoided certain people. I avoided areas of campus. I even avoided classes. Sometimes I needed to walk completely around campus to avoid walking straight to class if I believed I'd experience anxiety. I was afraid to see my friends. I was afraid to spend too much time with anyone, fearing bad thoughts or feelings would latch onto them. I couldn't watch television. I couldn't concentrate on my studies. I wasn't sleeping, so my running began to suffer. Everything was falling apart.

As I spiraled down, I tried so hard to maintain an image of perfection to the outside world. I invested every ounce of energy hiding my misery. Based on past experience, I knew this was just a bad cycle and it might end if I just held on. I did not want to taint the image I had built of myself in a moment of weakness. I needed to keep my façade intact because it was possible the cycle might break and I would be fine. I put on a happy face whenever I was around anyone. I pretended I was the normal, upbeat, enthusiastic Chrissie despite how draining it was. I hated myself. I hated how fake I was. I hated who I had to be to disguise this. I wished I could be anyone other than me.

I continued talking to Steve long-distance, desperately holding onto him as hope and reassurance. Talking to him helped me remember the days at camp when I felt better. I didn't want to lose that. I was also holding onto Jacob in order to prove my attraction against the bad thoughts. In truth, I didn't want either of them. I wanted to be alone. I wanted to run somewhere far away where no one knew me. I wanted to leave this tortured life and never think about it again. I dreamed of escaping, but knew that wasn't an option. I had to stay, and so I needed to create the best possible scenario to get me through it.

I didn't feel alive anymore. I had no idea who I was or who I wanted to be. I was alone. I watched my friends with envy as they laughed and lived their lives. I wanted to tell them. I wanted them to help me. I wanted to spill these worries and fears I battled every moment to someone just to get them out of my head. But I was terrified if I told anyone, it would mean the thoughts were true. If I told anyone, did it mean I had to start dating women? I couldn't do that. I didn't want that. I was trapped. I feared the bad thoughts and feelings would never go away. This episode lasting so long proved the thoughts would always return no matter what I did. I just wanted to know something. I wanted to know anything. But, all I had was uncertainty. My whole life had been driven, consumed, and engulfed in uncertainty. It was never ending. All I wanted was a clear answer, but no answers were ever good enough.

I began to believe it would never be better. My hope that this cycle would break began diminishing. I never experienced this amount of time or intensity with bad thoughts before, proving this was the worst it had ever been. It seemed death was the only acceptable answer. I knew the time was near. I had promised myself long ago if it came to a point when the cycle did not break, I would end my life.

Now I could see the writing on the wall. The time had come. It was time to die.

Chapter 15: Is Fear Enough to Stay Alive?

I heard the term 'depression' before, but never presumed it could happen to someone like me. I assumed it was a condition weak people experienced. Depressed people were just 'sad' about life and needed to snap out of it. But, I had no idea I was spiraling quickly and deeply into clinical depression. How could I know this? I spent the previous twelve years battling waves of misery associated with whether or not I would throw up or whether or not I had to turn gay. How would I know this could lead to actual depression? This was the only perspective I knew. This was how I saw, heard, and experienced the world. This was my life, and the only way I knew to experience it. This was the hand I was dealt. How could I know things differently? The only way I knew to perceive the world was through my own eyes. These eyes saw the same things every single day. It never occurred to me my brain could affect how situations or circumstances were perceived and reacted upon based on an imbalance. All I knew was what I saw, what I felt, and how to control it to the best of my ability. At age twenty, this was what I was given and how I handled it. How could I be expected to know the way I saw, experienced, and perceived the world was incorrect?

If only I had known, how differently things might have turned out.

My world became darker every day. Escape seemed impossible. My once perfectly held together life began slipping. I stopped caring more than I stopped trying. My energy reserves were depleted. The deep-seated anger took the reins of my thoughts and actions. Where most of my time and energy was spent doing the right thing to avoid exactly where I had now ended up, I began to realize what a waste it had all been. I couldn't pinpoint anything I had done wrong to deserve this punishment and frankly, I was tired of trying to be perfect for God. I didn't care what He thought anymore. I began to think He was a real jerk to yank me around by the torturous leash with which He held me. I didn't care what the hell I did or didn't do

anymore. There was no point anyway because I always ended up being punished. I could never do enough 'right' to make things okay and tolerable.

I stopped studying. Unable to concentrate for more than a few minutes, it seemed pointless to even try. I stopped caring about cross-country. I stopped hanging around friends. I made excuses about being tired in order to be alone. Everything I had built was falling apart. I wasn't surprised by my lack of energy because I had weathered these storms before. But the lack of interest in caring was different this time. Fear was the only emotion keeping me alive. Fear is a complex emotion. Its entrapment is terrifying, but its complexity allows you to 'feel' something disguised as hope. As long as I felt fear, I wouldn't feel numb. As long as I didn't feel completely numb, I could hold onto hope this cycle would break.

Losing my empathetic and sympathetic behaviors began to worry me. I stopped caring about anything and anyone around me. I stopped feeling emotions unassociated with anger or fear. Apathy and indifference seeped through my soul, like a slow infection. It was crippling me fatally. I wanted relief, but felt comfortable in the misery. I felt secure in my position of anger and resentment toward the lost years, and I was too tired to fight for emotions and feelings I wasn't sure would ever return.

I feared the possibility of never recovering. I always knew there was a possibility the cycle might not break, but was it finally here? I wanted the pain to end, but was yet sure I was ready to die. I still believed I wanted to live. I wanted to believe there was a different life for me. I wanted to believe I could move past this. I wanted to believe I could wake up and it would all be gone. I wanted to experience love. I wanted to laugh. I wanted to explore the world. I wanted to find out who Chrissie really was outside this madness. There were so many beautiful and wonderful things in the world I wanted to experience. *Why can't I stay for a little longer? Why does it have to be now? Why can't I focus on all of the great things and people in my life and overcome this? What can I do to be free from this misery?*

A continual dialogue began on whether this was the time to die. *How long will this go on before I take action? Am I nearing the end? What sort of sign do I need to see or feel to know this is it?* Finals were approaching and afterward I would be going home to Marietta for over a month for Christmas break. *Can I survive a month of down time feeling this way without distraction?* I committed to taking the month of November to decide what to do. *Maybe it will break? If not, will I need to make a suicide plan? Will I be okay?* I didn't know. Fear was evident. I wanted to hope things would be better, but I was too tired and worn down to think about anything other than a way out. Suicide seemed to be the only way.

My world evolved into a cyclic dialogue of confusion and misery. A record player in my mind evoked constant doubt. Everywhere I looked, something warped into questions of proof or disproof, challenging my character and morality. Something I saw would appeal to me, but the anxiety threw a question of doubt accusing my interpretation of being incorrect. The thoughts and fears were not only disturbing, they made me feel incompetent. I was giving power to thoughts I knew were not true, but the worry was more powerful than rationale. It didn't make sense. I felt like an idiot who could not figure out how to put a plug into an outlet to make the light come on. Every day I felt weaker, dumber, and more ashamed.

I detested looking at my face. The mirror revealed a monster. I stared into my green eyes wondering why I couldn't control this nonsense. I saw my face, I heard my voice, but they didn't match the person having the horrible thoughts. This monster inside me enfolded claws around my brain. The harder I fought, screamed, and cried, the harder it grasped, squeezed, twisted, and laughed at my misery. As much as I wanted to blame it on something else, I believed I was the cause. God let me know the consequences of my actions. When I sinned, He punished. As unfair as it seemed, it was my life. I wished I knew what I had done so wrong this time to make Him so angry. Now, there was no escape. This was the longest and most difficult episode of my life, and I couldn't see God's forgiveness in the near future.

As much as I tried to hold onto hope, I was afraid it was time to start planning suicide.

Chapter 16: Goodbye Friends

November tormented me. I waited patiently in agony praying for the cycle to break. I could feel myself sinking deeper into a dark hole. I tried to keep my eye focused on the fading light, begging and pleading with God to have mercy on me. I wanted to know the answer by the end of the month, but the more I searched the farther away resolution seemed.

Mama and I visited my sister in New York City for Thanksgiving. I hoped a change of scenery in the busiest city in America would instill hope and renew my energy. It had the opposite effect. I barely spoke to my sister and mama, claiming stress for upcoming finals as an excuse. I stayed in my sister's apartment to 'study' while they went to see the sights. I spent hours alone crying and praying for relief. There wasn't a moment's reprieve from the spinning thoughts. My body felt on fire as I reacted to everyone and everything.

I stood on the sidewalk one evening in Manhattan, watching hundreds of people walking by while mama and Joy stepped into a clothing store. I had never felt so alone. There were people all around me, even bumping into me, and I felt like a lost soul on this planet. I felt like an alien. I would give anything to trade places with any one of the people on the street. I was losing all hope and will to live.

Back at school, my cross-country season finished with disappointing statistics. I lost the drive and energy to care about doing well. My grades were the worst in my academic career. I barely held any information in my mind for finals. I avoided social activities the week before Christmas break, making excuses about being tired and stressed. Every spare minute was spent in bed curled in a fetal position. I didn't care what anyone thought anymore. I wanted to be invisible.

After my last final, I went to the sorority house to say goodbye to my friends heading home. Everyone was excited to see their families for the holidays. I felt sad and jealous. I went to my room, shut the door, and climbed under the covers. I stared out the window at the Pi Kappa Phi house, watching the fraternity boys packing their cars. My pillow quickly became soaked with tears. *Why can't I just be like everyone else? Why do I have to deal with this? What did I do so wrong to deserve this? I'm doing everything in my power to be the best Christian and I have fallen from grace so low and far there is no way to climb back into God's love and affection. I am a disappointment. I am an embarrassment.*

Laughter from across the street broke my train of thought. I turned to see men high-fiving, laughing, and having fun. *How could they be doing everything right and I am doing everything wrong? Doesn't anyone else get punished the way I do, or do they just hide it well? What have I done wrong?*

I buried my head in my pillow and cried for the bad person I must be. I cried for the good person I knew I could never be. I cried believing all the good I had done until a few months ago was in vain. I cried because I couldn't understand why other people did whatever they wanted without experiencing any punishment. I cried because I believed this would be the last time I saw any of my friends at Georgia Southern. I cried even harder knowing no one knew it would be the last time. I cried because no one could save me. It was my duty to end my life. I was taught if you did not have God, you had nothing. This was obviously my reality. God had abandoned me, so now I had nothing. All hope of this breaking had vanished. As I wiped my eyes, I felt them glaze over with indifference.

I needed to not care. I had nothing to hold onto. I couldn't live feeling this way anymore. I had no energy or strength. I had no hope. I needed to kill myself over Christmas break. I knew I did not want to die, but living this way was excruciating. I only saw darkness. It was a dull ache. I was numb. I was empty. It took effort to breathe. I was exhausted but couldn't sleep. Sleep would give me an escape, but it eluded me. The depression was inescapable.

I needed to make a plan.

A jolt of fear and panic surged through me at the thought of suicide. I sat up. My breathing increased. I felt hot and tingly as if the thoughts were happening. I jumped to my feet pacing and packing to distract myself. I wanted to run. *I can't make this decision now, can I? I will give it to God. I will ask God to give me a clear sign in the next twenty-four hours if He believes I should kill myself. That's it! I will use the time for Him to let me know what to do. This way I can trust Him to make the decision. He will see how strong my faith is, have mercy on me, and relieve this horrible episode.*

My anxiety decreased just by making this plan with God. If there were no clear signs in twenty-four hours, I needed to hang on longer. I relaxed. The temporary relief gave me motivation to pack my bags and head downstairs to say goodbye to my friends.

I dropped my bags into the trunk and glanced up at my bedroom. Shading my eyes from the sun, I squinted to see into the window. I imagined myself lying on the bed, clutching my pillow while crying, staring back and waving goodbye. A shiver went up my spine.

I wondered if I would ever look out that window again. I wondered if I would see the inside of the sorority house again. The decision was up to God now. I had to concentrate on finding a sign from Him over the next twenty-four hours. I hoped this was the ultimate act of faith. Perhaps I could win back His favor by trusting Him. I held that belief the entire ride home. But, any shred of hope faded as I pulled into my neighborhood. Memories of bad thoughts in high school began flooding my brain. This must be proof. This must be the sign. The fact I still have bad thoughts after all the years must be proof it will never go away. I prayed silently for God to intervene and save me from this proof, but felt no relief. The burden of proof sat squarely on my shoulders to bear. I couldn't feel God anywhere near me. I was alone again.

My anxiety increased rapidly the closer I got to my house. Mama greeted me at the door with a hug. I strained to keep from bursting into tears. She scurried to the kitchen rattling on about dinner and weekend plans. I stood in the foyer, staring into the living room still clutching my bags. The familiar feelings of bad thoughts during high school rushed in. I fixated on the feeling that nothing had changed since the first day the obsessions showed up. It would never get better. I felt the weight of anxiety heavy on my shoulders. My energy was so depleted, I couldn't react. I stood still and let it beat me all over. I believed I deserved the punishment. I could barely breathe. I was paralyzed.

Mama poked her head around the corner, snapping me into reality. "Are you hungry? How was your trip? Did you do well on your finals?"

"Not really. Fine. Yea, I guess," I said. "I'm tired. I'm going to lie down."

"Well, 20/20 comes on soon. We can watch it while we eat."

I turned down the hallway toward my bedroom. It looked exactly the same as when I left for college. How badly I wanted to rewind life and leave for college again. I longed to be that person again. I was scared she was gone forever. I couldn't imagine things would get better. I only had two options. I could tell someone and be forced to live a life I didn't want to. Or I could kill myself. I was unhappy with either choice. I hated myself. I hated how weak and stupid I was for being unable to handle this. I believed I was a disgrace to God with this magnitude of punishment. I believed I deserved to die.

I threw my bags on the floor, falling face first onto the bed. I was trapped with no routine or distraction for six weeks. The house reminded me things would never be different or better for me. The old argument in my head surfaced. *If I'm not supposed to be gay, I wouldn't still be worrying about it after all these years?* I closed my eyes tightly as the tears welled up. I wished I was just gay and in the closet and could come out already! I wished I was just scared and trapped in the closet, too afraid to tell anyone. At least I would know with certainty what this was all about. I knew it wasn't that simple. There was something else I couldn't figure out. I was so tired of searching for answers I would never find.

Mama hollered at me from the living room that it was time to eat. I sat up and wiped my face with my jacket. I changed into pajamas and took a deep breath before walking down the hallway. She brought me a plate of food. I avoided eating by pushing everything around, taking small bites, and chewing each bite for a long time. I put my plate down as the music for 20/20 started. Words flashed across the screen and I froze in my chair. My head heated up and became covered in goose-bumps. A lump of heat burned in my stomach and began moving into my chest and spine approaching my neck.

"Tonight on 20/20, special in-depth coverage: Lesbians in their 50's"

I couldn't move. I was paralyzed with fear. Mama mumbled something about the title, but I couldn't hear her over the thundering heartbeat echoing in my ears. My reality began fading away from the television set. I wanted to run screaming from the house. I needed fresh air, but I didn't want mama to know what was happening. *If I'm reacting this way, isn't that proof I am supposed to be gay? If there wasn't some truth to it, I wouldn't even care about this stupid story on 20/20, right?*

I watched two lesbians in their fifties hold hands while smiling and talking to the camera. I was in such a state of panic I couldn't hear anything they were saying. I did everything possible to control the waves of panic.

This is the sign. Why would this particular show be airing tonight if God didn't want me to see it? Is this what is going to happen to me in 30 years? Did these ladies worry about whether or not they had to be gay when they were my age? I can't believe this! I do not want to be with women! WHY do I have to be if I don't want to?

As the initial shock faded I heard the sound of the TV ringing in my ears. I heard the fifty-year-old lesbian say, "I was married for twenty-five years, then one day I was singing in the church choir, and looked over and saw Judy looking at me, and well, it was love at first sight!"

OH MY GOD! IS THIS WHAT IS GOING TO HAPPEN TO ME!? IS ALL THIS THE PRECURSOR WORRY TO THE FACT THAT I WILL BE THIS WOMAN ONE DAY?

I excused myself to the bathroom to privately panic, closed the door, and held onto the bathroom sink. I could hardly breathe. The fact I was reacting this way to the 'Lesbians in their 50's' story *must be a sign I have to be gay. Anyone truly straight wouldn't let something like those lesbians make their entire body react this way, would they? What was the answer?* I looked at my face in the mirror. It was red, blotchy, and streaked with tears. I searched my eyes for what to do. *Should I keep waiting it out to see if it will break? I'm so scared to kill myself. What if I fail? What if I don't succeed and end up paralyzed or permanently injured? What if someone finds me before I die and I have to tell them why I am killing myself?* I wanted to slam my head into the mirror and break the glass. I hated looking at myself. *Who the hell am I? What did I do to deserve this?*

In a few minutes I calmed down. I closed my eyes picturing Judy and her lesbian partner holding hands and smiling at the camera. They were so happy being lesbians. I could not imagine being happy holding a woman's hand. This isn't what I wanted. This doesn't make sense to me. *Did Judy know she wanted to date women, ever? What if Judy worried like I did when she was my age, and then was forced to date women and now likes it?*

I hated Judy and her lesbian lover. I hated 20/20. I hated God for putting me in this position. And, I hated myself. *I must be the worst person on the planet to deserve this misery.* God grants good to good people, and God punishes those that are evil. *Well, DAMN YOU GOD! I have begged you. I have pleaded with you to have mercy on me. I have done everything I could possibly think of to be good in your eyes. I have been the best Christian in order to make the bad thoughts go away, yet you still punish me.*

I no longer want to love you, God. I no longer want to trust you, God. I will no longer serve you, God. I will end my life. I will take control. I have given up all control to you, and you have given me nothing but fear and misery. I will take this in my own hands and no longer allow you to control me.

With that prayer, I decided to kill myself. I only needed to figure out how and when. The logistics would be the hard part, but I felt a rush of relief knowing it would soon be over. There was a moment of reprieve knowing the pain would end. No one would ever know my horrible thoughts. No one would find out what a disappointment I was. No one would find out what a horrible person I was on the inside.

The decision was made.

Chapter 17: The How and When of Suicide

I pulled the covers to my chin still shaken about lesbian Judy, but partly relieved knowing it would soon be over. The bright red numbers on the clock read 10:56pm. I wanted sleep so badly. I needed it. My depressive state wasn't allowing me to get sufficient rest. I drifted in and out, and was jerked out of sleep after 4:00am. I sat up and looked at the clock. The anxiety felt like a freight train hitting me from behind. I bent over in agony. Uncontrollable, intrusive thoughts raced through my mind. Panic ensued regarding suicide. My mind felt on fire. I wanted it to stop. I wanted to scream, but if I did mama would know something was wrong.

I sat bent over, clutching my legs for two hours paralyzed with thoughts. I heard mama stirring in the house before 7:00am. I was excruciatingly tired. I swung my legs off the bed and gave myself a pep talk about being fake happy in front of mama. She was leaving early and would be gone until later in the evening. So I was stuck in the house all day by myself. I was glad not to pretend to be happy all day, but felt scared to be alone with my thoughts. It felt dangerous and unstable. I had no clue how to tell mama any of this.

Mama rushed out of the house, and I dragged myself to the couch. Everything on TV triggered me. Every person appearing on the screen prompted my brain to find proof if I was attracted to them. It didn't matter if it was man, woman, child, or animal, I couldn't figure out who or what I was attracted to. I experienced anxiety looking at every living mammal crossing the screen. I felt the arousal reaction to everything and everyone. It was stupidly irrational and confusing, but convincing enough for me to stay in the cycle. I was too tired to fight back with mental rituals, so I just surrendered to the misery.

It will all be over soon.

I stayed in this daze for seven hours before realizing if I wanted to get in a run, I needed to hurry before dark. Running was a release for me, so I hoped it would help with my suicide thoughts. I laced up my Adidas and headed to the sidewalk. Normally my head cleared 10 minutes into exercise, but today I noticed the anxiety and brain chattering felt more intense the more my feet pounded the pavement. I rounded the corner of a large intersection and increased my pace hoping to find relief, but couldn't keep my breath. The anxiety was overwhelming. My heart beat intensely in my throat. I slowed to a gangly walk and then stopped. I bent over onto the sidewalk, squatted down, grabbed my running shoes, and began sobbing heavily. My only outlet was taken away. If I could not run and find relief, nothing would help me now. I stood up in defeat, turned around and slowly walked home, crying the entire way.

I knew it was time to make a suicide plan. But with the intense thoughts plaguing me, I couldn't concentrate. I tried distracting myself with TV but could barely focus on any shows. Thirsty, I jumped from the couch quickly turning toward the kitchen. I arose too fast, my head felt fuzzy, and my vision blurred. I bent over, resting my hands on my knees. As my vision started clearing, so did the fog in my head. I swung around, looking at the kitchen. It looked different. I could see color. I felt different. *Could this episode be breaking?* I felt my stomach aching from hunger. I grabbed chicken out of the fridge and devoured it. I could taste! I was starving! I was elated!

I jumped on the couch, clicking through channels. There was no anxiety! The clouds had parted in my mind and light was shining inside me again. *Could it be I had been tested to see if I'd actually go through with the suicide? Was this God's way of seeing how far I would go? Am I like Abraham and Isaac when God tested whether or not Abraham would kill his son, Isaac? Did I pass the test? God, are you still there?*

I listened to my answering machine I had ignored all day. There were messages from Steve wanting to see me. I was excited to call him back. Was this proof? Oh I didn't care, I was just so happy I could see, hear, and feel again. We talked for a couple hours and made plans to see each other the next day. I was relieved I did not have to complete suicide now! Thank goodness I waited to make the plan. This had been the longest and worst cycle by far. I hoped it would never get this bad again, but at least I now knew I was able to endure absolute misery until it broke.

I couldn't wait to finally get a decent night's sleep. I would wake up in the morning fresh and renewed with a positive outlook on life. The next day I would be able to put all that had happened behind me. My head hit the pillow with a big smile of relief on my face. The bright, red numbers on the clock read 11:33pm.

My eyes opened to the bright, red numbers reading 4:38am. I sat up and felt the anxiety completely take over my head. The anxiety about both the gay thoughts and suicide was overwhelming. My hands and chest began shaking uncontrollably. I couldn't breathe. I was drowning. I lay down, tried to catch my breath and prayed to go back to sleep. *Is this a bad dream? Is it possible I could have done something wrong since last night to offend God? Did I sin in my sleep? Did I think something wrong that offended God? Why am I experiencing this again? I thought it had broken?* My tears were out of control.

Why does this happen to me? Why can't I just be normal? Am I the only person dealing with these issues? What have I done to deserve this punishment?

Crying and praying in agony, I desperately tried to pinpoint what I had done wrong. The cumulative loss of sleep affected my ability to fight the anxiety. I stared at the bright, red numbers on the clock slowly turning over every minute. I wanted the sun to come up. There was no hope in the darkness.

The clock read 8:00am when I heard mama moving around in her room. I questioned how I would muster strength to get through church. The house of the Lord was the last place I wanted to be. I knew He did not want me there. He hated me. He must be ashamed of me allowing this misery to continue. I got up begrudgingly. I avoided seeing mama until we left the house. I didn't have the energy to fake being happy anymore.

We drove to the Elizabeth Methodist Church in Marietta, GA. I knew everyone would be excited to hear how wonderful life was at college. *How am I going to lie to all of these people?*

I was grateful to have an hour to myself once the service started. Mama was the pianist, and I sat two rows behind her. I could not make eye contact with the minister. I wondered if he knew how much God hated me. I wondered if he could see there was something evil inside of me. I kept my head lowered. Images of killing myself plagued my mind. I couldn't turn them off. I was suffocating. All I could see was blood. Sweat beads formed on my brow as I gripped the wooden pew with my fingernails.

As the singing of the final hymn echoed through the chapel, I felt the urge to cry. I failed at fighting the tears. They dripped down my face onto my Sunday dress. I ducked my head behind the hymnal.

I'm starting to lose it. I used to be able to control my emotions, but it's obvious I cannot anymore. I cannot go on like this. People will know something is wrong, and I won't be able to hide anymore.

Friends swarmed around me after the benediction inquiring about my emotional breakdown. I lied, saying it had been a stressful quarter at school. They bought my excuse while hugging and telling me they'd pray for me to have strength and healing. I smiled and agreed. Indeed strength and healing was what I needed for sure.

Mama and I went to The Golden Corral for Sunday lunch. It was painful forcing conversation in the car and at the restaurant. Images of driving off a cliff in my car plagued my mind. Visions of wounding myself with a knife were prevalent. They were terrifying, but comforting. Mama was oblivious to my distance. I nodded and replied blandly to her conversations, while suicidal thoughts stole every moment. Every few minutes, I felt panic believing this was really the time to turn to suicide. I sweated and breathed heavily, as my hands became tingly and numb. I searched the restaurant for the nearest exit in case I needed to bolt. I couldn't let mama see the panic.

Am I really going to do this? Is this really happening? Am I really going through with this?

Suicidal visualizations consumed me all afternoon. Arriving home, I excused myself to my room saying I was 'tired'. Mama wanted me to attend a concert she was singing in later. I was also supposed to drive to Carrollton to meet Steve. *How am I going to make it through tonight with these uncontrollable thoughts? I know I can't make excuses forever.* I wanted to see Steve, but was afraid I wouldn't be able to act 'normal'. *What if he suspects something?*

I couldn't excuse myself from attending mama's concert without her suspecting something was wrong, so I agreed to go. I sat in the parking lot watching the sun set behind the trees before going inside. I wanted to run as far away from my life as I could. *My life is miserable. I hate who I am. I don't deserve a good life, and this is why God is punishing me.*

The clock turned to 5:00pm, and I needed to go inside. I popped the visor mirror down to clean off the mascara streaming down my face. I barely recognized myself in the mirror. I looked sick. I wiped my face attempting to create the façade I had lived by for so long. Entering the auditorium, I headed toward the least crowded area. But before I knew it, seats around me began filling up. As I started gathering my things to move somewhere less crowded, a young woman sat down beside me. I didn't think it would be polite to move after she sat down, and I began to panic. I couldn't look at her.

Why did she have to sit beside me? What if I think she is attractive? Did she think I sent out a vibe I was gay so she sat here? What if I look at her wrong and she thinks I am hitting on her? Why do I have these thoughts if I'm really not gay? Straight people don't worry about these things, right? Oh my God, help.

I was afraid to look at her. *What if I look in her direction and think she is attractive? Would that be proof? What if I accidentally brush her leg or something and she thinks I'm hitting on her?* I felt the bad physical feelings and thoughts. *I need to get the hell out of here now, but what if I brush up against her on the way out and like it? Or, what if she thinks I'm brushing up against her on purpose?* My panic came to a halt when she turned and asked me if I had ever heard this chorus before.

"…um…uh…yea….my mom sings soprano," I answered carefully without looking in her direction.

She responded with small talk about a friend she knew in the choir. I took a deep breath slowly turning my head in her direction, carefully monitoring any movement or response of my body and mind to find proof or disproof. She asked me questions and as I began to answer more enthusiastically, I noticed my mind begin to separate from the fog. As I talked with her, the room opened around me and a weight rose off me. My vision was peripheral. I could hear conversations. I could see colors. I could relax my body and breathe normally. It felt like the day before when I thought the episode had broken.

Maybe this time is real? Maybe God needed to get one more test of faith from me. Maybe He just wanted to see how much pain I could take to prove I trusted Him?

The concert began and the choir music felt as if it were being sung for me. I had made it through another day. I felt the harmony of the hymns coursing through my veins. I silently thanked God for the chance He was giving me. I needed to keep faith and believe He would always protect me. How could I have lost sight of that? He would always deliver me from the evil. I just needed to have more faith.

After the concert, I ran to the stage to hug mama goodbye. I was eager to see Steve now the cycle had broken again. The timing was perfect. Being with him would make me feel even more confident of the worst being over.

Driving down the highway at 75mph toward Carrollton, I approached a large overpass. My body began to react oddly. As I neared the overpass, I visualized slamming my car into the concrete pillars. I worried I wouldn't be able to stop myself from doing it. My hands gripped the steering wheel so tightly my knuckles ached. I began sweating and breathing heavily. I suddenly felt out of control.

Should I stop the car? What if I cannot control myself from running off the road? Because I'm thinking this, does this mean I want to run into the pillar? What if I cannot stop it? Am I going to do it? Should I do it? What does this mean? Does this prove it is time to kill myself? Is this the way I should do it?

I closed my eyes as my car sped under the bridge. A shiver went through my spine, and radiated through my body. Gasping for breath, I noticed my chest and arms were shaking violently. I slowed down, and pulled to the side of the road. I rocked back and forth and tried to stop myself from shaking. I was sobbing and screaming at the top of my lungs at God.

"WHY IS THIS HAPPENING TO ME!? WHAT DO YOU WANT FROM ME? YOU ARE AN AWFUL GOD TO DO THIS TO ME! WHY DO YOU WANT ME DEAD? WHAT DID I DO SO HORRIBLE TO OFFEND YOU THAT YOU CONTINUE TO DO THIS TO ME?????"

It took a half hour to calm down. With only 15 minutes to Steve's house, I needed to pull myself together before I saw him. No one could know about this. I began driving again, and barely drove over 40mph out of fear. Just seeing an oncoming underpass caused me to panic and shake.

Is this a sign I should kill myself now? Why am I reacting physically if there is not some truth behind the thought? This is not the way I would choose, but something is obviously telling me to since I am reacting this way. Right?

I made a commitment not to slam into a concrete pillar that night, but I needed to find some sort of proof if this was how I had to die. I didn't believe I was ready to go through with it, especially since it seemed as if things had broken only hours before.

I pulled into Steve's driveway and saw the back door open. I was so glad to see his face. *What would he think of me if he knew I might slam into a concrete pillar soon?* He embraced me with a huge hug and the weight of worry fell off me. I walked into the kitchen to see Zeke, another friend from camp, who greeted me with a hug. I wanted to cry with gratitude. Two people who reminded me of who I was outside of this mess welcomed me with open arms. Feelings of camp nostalgia surfaced filling me with relief. I was safe. I decided to make a plan in the morning, but for now I would enjoy being around them.

Steve and Zeke played their guitars and sang for a bit. It brought me close to tears remembering last summer when things made sense. We reminisced about camp. We told funny stories and laughed all evening. The distraction was a blessing. I so badly wanted to tell them what was happening. I knew I was their friend and they would listen. I desperately wanted to ask them for help. I wanted to tell them I didn't want to die. But, I was scared of what they would do if they found out. I was scared they would think I was crazy. I was scared they would hate me or judge me. I recognized this might be my last chance to ask for help, but I couldn't do it. I looked at them and stopped the words from coming out of my mouth. I prevented myself from telling them, and breaking down in front of them. I pretended to be happy. I pretended to be normal. I kept smiling, laughing, and faking everything was alright.

A deep, penetrating fear was taking over. I believed the proof I experienced in the car meant suicide was inevitable. I could not hold on any longer. I was plagued with images and physical reactions, so it must be real. The fear tied itself to my feet like a weight, and I pictured sinking to the bottom of a lake, drowning as I watched the light of the world fade away above me. At this moment, my life on earth depended only on how long I could hold my breath.

Chapter 18: The Pact with God

I stood at the kitchen door in the morning looking back at Steve and Zeke. I could barely bring myself to say goodbye. I wanted to tell them this would be the last time I laid eyes on them. I wanted to tell them how thankful I was spending last evening wrapped in the safety of their friendship. I wanted to tell them how sorry I was for what would soon happen to me. I swallowed the lump in my throat as I told Steve I would see him in a week or so. It was hard lying to him. I knew I'd never see him again. I barely looked either of them in the face as I turned to leave for fear they would see straight through me.

My heart ached leaving my friends as I cranked the car and backed down the driveway. I was headed to my dad and stepmom's house. Linda, my stepmom, had secured a temp job for me at the Coca-Cola office over Christmas break. I was not excited about this since I had no energy or drive to do anything. Being anywhere in public was agonizing. I didn't want to talk to anyone, much less try to do a temp job around people I didn't know. I dreaded starting the next day. *Will I kill myself before I start? When will I know the right time to complete suicide?*

The drive to daddy's house was torture. Even though I had decided not to smash into an overpass, I cringed and ruminated at every passing. I was terrified of losing control and doing it. *If I do it, what will happen if the impact doesn't kill me? What if I'm only injured or disfigured? I'll still be alive with these fears. I can't take the risk.*

I couldn't stop thinking about suicide. How and when to kill myself was on my mind every minute. I had never experienced such a state of intense and urgent fear. There were no answers or reasons. It was just there, and there was no stopping it. I couldn't outthink it or outsmart it. Everywhere I looked presented an opportunity to kill myself. It was frightening.

I arrived safely in Fairburn and immediately retired to my room because of how 'tired' I was from finals. I spent hours ruminating on ways kill myself around daddy's house. There was a lake at a park nearby. I fixated on an image of a large stone tied to my feet, dragging me to the bottom of the lake and keeping me there until I drowned. I pictured what I would see from the bottom of the lake as I took my last breath. I couldn't shake the image. When I thought about it for too long, I started breathing heavily and my chest and arms shook. *Is this reaction a 'sign' of the way I should die?*

The misery of working at a temp job with people I didn't know plagued me as well. *What if I break down in front of these people? What if the bad thoughts and physical reactions start and I cannot escape?* The desire to die was becoming urgent. Thoughts of death brought relief. In my mind, I was already walking dead. I felt numb. I wasn't happy. I wasn't sad. I wasn't angry. I wasn't anything. I did not even feel afraid anymore.

I was empty. I was hopeless. I was absolutely alone. It was over for me.

I set my alarm for 5:00am, but didn't need it. I wasn't sleeping anymore. I stayed up all night thinking about dying in the water. I had no idea whether or not I would go to Heaven or Hell if I committed suicide, and I didn't care. Anything would be better than this all-consuming misery. I wanted it to be over. I decided tomorrow I would make a solid plan and an exact time to do it. I was tired of waiting and anticipating. My life was over. All that was left was to destroy the shell of this person I walked around in. Nothing about the person inside of that shell mattered anymore. I drifted into light sleep after making the decision. I had no prayers or pleas to ask of God. I couldn't care less what He thought anymore.

Lack of sleep compounded my state of depression. I barely spoke to Linda on the way to work. My eyes fixated on the five story concrete parking garage as we pulled into the Coca-Cola building. *There is no way I could survive the fall off the top level.* As we drove up the structure, my adrenalin began to pump.

This could be it. This could be the solution.

After entering the building, Linda pointed me in the right direction and we made a plan to meet for lunch. I wondered if I would still be alive at noon.

I found I was working the letter stamping machine all day. The thought of standing in one place under fluorescent lights listening to a loud machine all day made me feel nauseous. I gritted my teeth, put my head down, and got to work. I couldn't get my mind off the parking garage. *What if I jumped and survived? Would it make a mess when I hit the ground? What if someone saw me and tried to stop me?* The questions consumed me for hours. Before I knew it, it was time to meet Linda for lunch.

We headed to the cafeteria. I grabbed a tray of food and sat across from her. I pushed the food around barely eating anything, and then she said it.

"You don't seem to be eating much these days, I've noticed. Is everything okay?"

I panicked. *What should I say?* It was noticeable to me, but wasn't sure anyone else knew. I had probably dropped two sizes in the past month. I desperately wanted to tell her. I wanted to scream and cry and describe the misery I had lived with for twelve years. I wanted to tell her everything and hear her say it would be okay. I wanted to say out loud I wanted to kill myself only to experience the relief of releasing the fear by putting it into words. I wanted to tell her how I couldn't stop thinking about jumping off the top of the parking garage.

But I didn't.

"I'm fine. I'm just really tired lately and I think it's affecting my appetite," I said without looking at her for fear of crying.

She had a look that communicated she didn't believe me. I dropped my head forcing a few bites of chicken sandwich to prove I was telling the truth. She didn't respond. I was happy not to explain further, but something inside of me wished she had pushed the issue.

I begrudgingly headed to the basement after lunch. I knew if something was going to happen on that parking structure, it needed to happen soon. I went to the manager and asked if I was going to have a break in the afternoon. He told me I had a fifteen minute break at 3:00pm. That was it, the time I would jump off the top floor of the parking garage. There was no way I could stop it now. I anxiously watched the hands of the clock tick off every minute leading to 3:00pm.

The clock struck three, and I watched the manager coming to relieve me. I told him I would be back in a few minutes, but was lying. I headed to the large, bright lobby, out the glass doors, and toward the parking garage. I walked up the stairs to the exposed top floor. My legs and arms felt numb. I stepped onto the empty top floor of the garage. I circled the entire lot and ended up on the side facing the lobby I had just walked out of. Leaning over the edge seeing how far the ground was, I felt certain it would be a miracle if I survived the fall. But of course, doubt lingered. *What if I survived? What if I broke my neck, but still had to occupy my mind?* I knew my rational mind was trying to talk me out of jumping, and I needed to silence it. It was time to die.

The railing was out of reach, so I climbed onto the hood of the car next to it. I held onto a pillar connecting the walls and leaned over. My heart jumped from the rush of adrenalin. I pulled myself back. *Does this have to be the end? How did I get here? What did I do so wrong to deserve this life?*

I looked at the people walking obliviously in and out of the Coca-Cola building. They had no idea I was standing five stories up waiting to die. *No one has to deal with the crap I have been through for twelve years. WHY? I must be a failure to God. I must be a disappointment to God. I wish I could be any one of those people in the Coca-Cola building. I wish I could be anyone but me.*

My legs and arms were shaking. The opportunity was passing. I knelt on the ledge, wrapped my arms around my legs, and looked to the sky. I could see for miles into the horizon. A few lazy clouds drifted across the sky as the sun made its way westward. I began sobbing.

I screamed into the sky;

"DO YOU REALLY WANT ME TO DO THIS? IS THIS WHAT YOU REALLY WANT, GOD? I DON'T WANT TO DIE, BUT I BELIEVE IT IS THE ONLY CHOICE I HAVE! TELL ME WHAT YOU WANT ME TO DO!"

I dropped my head, crying into my lap. Taking a deep breath, I stood up straight, looked over onto the grass below, and looked into the sky again. Something inside me hesitated. I grabbed the pillar with my hand, slid my hands down it, and knelt down again.

Don't do it.

Not now.

Don't jump.

I hugged the pillar with all my strength and felt the cycle breaking. The fog lifted and I could see, hear, and smell everything around me. I looked at the sky and the drifting clouds seemed different. They were filled with pink and orange hues. They were beautiful.

I'm not going to die here. I'm not going to jump.

I swung around, jumped down onto the car, and back onto the floor of the garage. Breathing heavily and shaking all over, I stumbled down the stairs practically running to the basement. I was late, but I didn't care. I was alive and I wasn't going to die today. Once again, I held onto hope that maybe I was just being tested and it truly broke this time. I thanked God for His mercy, and prayed this feeling would stay with me. I asked forgiveness for everything and hoped He would give me another chance after all of the doubting I had done.

I descended the steps to the basement an entirely different person. It appeared as if the manager had never seen me before when I walked through the door. I was cheerful, happy, and gregarious. I chatted up everyone in the room for the remaining hour. I felt alive. I was absolutely sure the final test had been issued and I had passed. Things would get better now, I knew it.

I met Linda in front of the same doors of the Coca-Cola building I had exited earlier anticipating my death. We turned toward the parking garage, and I felt a shot of adrenalin. I ignored it, trying to hang onto the idea all misery was behind me now. As we got into the car, I noticed it was a bit awkward with Linda. I knew she was confused why I had so much to say now, when I have barely uttered a word in the last couple days. But, I ignored it and kept talking. There was no need to dwell in the miserable past or offer up explanations. I was elated the torture was over. I asked her if we could order pizza tonight. She agreed and let me know daddy was teaching Bible study at the church later if I wanted to go.

Of course I do! I owe everything to God for letting this break before I was about to end my life.

The three of us sat down to dinner and I couldn't eat fast enough. I hadn't eaten much in a few days, so I was starving. Daddy and Linda looked a bit stunned at my behavior. I knew it was confusing, but there was no need to explain now the bad episode was over. I blew it off and finished several pieces of pizza before daddy and I headed to the church.

There were eight of us sitting in a circle in the church classroom for Bible study. I sat across from daddy listening as he read the scripture we were discussing that evening. His voice started out strong and bold, but as he got farther into the passage, his voice began to fade. It felt as if someone were wrapping a rope around my stomach, pulling me away from the group. I could see daddy's lips moving, but I couldn't hear anything he was saying. My feet and hands felt like fire, and the heat slowly moved into my chest and neck. I tried to fight it, but the bad thoughts and physical feelings began creeping in. I was afraid I was suffocating, so I excused myself and sprinted to the bathroom. I slammed the door behind me, running into the bathroom stall. I put my cheek against the metal door trying to cool down. I slid down the side of the wall, squatting onto the floor, holding my knees, and burying my head in my lap. This is awful. It didn't break. It was back.

This makes no sense! I am in the church doing everything I am supposed to be doing to be a good Christian! How could I go back in there? All of those people are good Christians, and here I am being punished by the same God we are trying to learn about and worship! I am an incompetent moron. All I can think about is death in a room of Christian people. Daddy would be ashamed of me. I am an embarrassment. He is this incredible minister who does great things for people and who God absolutely adores. I am his stupid, idiot daughter who God has rejected; who cannot control her own thoughts; who contemplates killing herself every minute. How could he love me if he knew the truth? How could he forgive me for disappointing God? If he knew how much God was torturing me, he would know I deserved to be punished also. He would abandon me, too.

Tonight solidified it would be better for my family if I were dead. How disappointed would they be to learn the image of their daughter was a lie? What would they do if they learned I am so weak and stupid I cannot stop worrying about things that aren't even true?

They would be ashamed if they knew. They would be embarrassed. They would wish I was dead even if they didn't say it out loud. Their lives will be better without me. I would rather them remember me as who they think they know me to be than knowing the truth of how horrible I am.

Daddy saw through my excuses when I told everyone I was just tired and not feeling well. We drove home in silence. As we pulled into the driveway, he asked me if I was okay. I turned away so he couldn't see me lie to his face. I told him I was fine and just needed to get some sleep. He hesitated, and drove on.

I went straight to my room, got under the covers, and cried as quietly as possible. I heard the phone ring and then footsteps up the hallway. Daddy knocked at the door telling me Steve was on the phone. I told him to take a message. I heard him hesitate, wanting to say something to me, but he turned and walked back down the hall chatting with Steve.

I slid onto my knees at the side of the bed, clasped my hands together, and placed them on my forehead. I pleaded with God to have mercy. I begged Him to save me. I bargained with Him for whatever I could offer if He would just allow this episode to break for good.

And I made a deal with Him.

I could not do this roller-coaster ride anymore. I needed real proof, so I decided to take control. I made a pact with God. I told God I would trust Him in the decision to stay alive or die tonight. I would set my alarm for 5:00am. If He wanted me to kill myself, He would make sure I woke up before my alarm went off. If I didn't wake up before the alarm, I needed to continue to trust in a purpose and back off from planning my suicide. If I woke before 5:00am, I would know there was no hope and He wanted me to kill myself. The pact was the first time I felt I could rely on real answers instead of 'proof'. There would be a clear answer with no grey area.

I needed to prepare some things in case God wanted me to kill myself. I left a butcher knife behind the toaster so if God wanted me to die, I could grab it noiselessly. I cracked open the basement door in case I needed to leave without disturbing anyone. I laid out my Adidas, sweatshirt, and sweatpants by my bedroom door. I set my alarm for five, turned out the light, rolled over and stared out the window at the moonlight shining through the window. It never crossed my mind to leave a note.

I thought about my roommate, Allison. I hoped she would understand. Oh, how I would miss laughing with her. I thought about my cross-country team and how much fun we had the last few years. I thought about Brad. He was one of the best friends I had ever had. Thinking about him made me cry. I wanted to call him so badly and tell him everything. Out of anyone, I believed he would understand and accept me anyway. I thought about my family. As much as I wouldn't want them to be sad, I could only think how much better off they would be without me. Everything about me was a lie. How could they ever love me? I was beneath them. I was an embarrassment. They deserved a better daughter and sister. I was thinking about my loved ones when I started to doze off. I saw the bright, red digital lights turn to 11:00pm just before my eyes shut.

I woke up suddenly, out of breath. It was light outside! I leaned over, looking out the window anticipating sunlight only to discover the rays of the full moon were shining on my bed. My heart sank. I quickly shut my eyes hoping I wasn't fully awake, but it was too late.

I slowly rolled over to look at the clock. The bright, red digital lights read 2:05am. God had fulfilled His end of the bargain. I was sad and disappointed, but I knew what I had to do.

Chapter 19: In the Still of the Night

I was on autopilot. God told me what to do, so I obeyed. The bright, red digital numbers read 2:05am when I arose to put on the clothes I had laid by the door. I quietly opened my bedroom door, and tiptoed to the kitchen. I slid my hand behind the toaster oven until my finger touched the sharp blade. I traced the outside of the blade to the handle of the knife, grasped it, and tiptoed to the basement door. I stepped lightly down the creaky, wooden steps leading downstairs. I shuffled past the washer/dryer, heading toward the moonlight shining through the basement door I had left cracked open. As I approached the door, something reflected in the light. Our cat, Phoebe, was perched near the ceiling on top of old furniture. Our eyes met, and I felt a chill. It seemed as if she knew something bad was happening. I hesitated for a moment, then broke our gaze and pressed on.

I slipped through the open door and onto a small concrete patio. The cold air felt painful on my face. It took my breath away.

Good. The colder it is, the quicker this will end.

I headed through the front yard onto the street. I realized I was carrying the butcher knife in the open. I couldn't be seen walking down the street with this, so I slid it's blade into my sock, covering the handle with my sweatpants. I stumbled off the lawn onto the pavement underneath the streetlights. There was a peaceful ambience. The combination of cold air and humidity created floating crystals. It was like walking in a dream. With sparkles and glitter floating all around me, it was as if I were the only person awake in that moment. I was in a spotlight. I wanted to stay in that moment forever.

I walked through my sparkly spotlight down the street, looking at the neighbor's houses. They were probably sleeping soundly, warm in their beds. Did they have any idea outside their house tonight, someone was about to die? Did they know how stupid, weak and what a disappointment this person was? Did they know this someone did not deserve to experience love, warmth, or acceptance? Did these neighbors know how lucky they were to have the life they had?

I took a right turn at the end of the street and crossed to the other side. I walked through a large yard, and then saw it. A small creek bed I believed was deep enough for what needed to happen. I approached the edge, looking into the water. I couldn't turn back now. I stumbled down the muddy bank.

I stepped one foot into the water. It took about ten seconds for the water to soak into my Adidas. I underestimated how cold the water would be. The chill shot up into my chest, taking my breath away.

I put my second foot in the water hoping it would feel different, but it was just as painful. I dropped my knees into the water. It quickly soaked through my sweatpants. The magnitude of pain from the water on my skin felt unbearable, like being stabbed all over my legs. I couldn't decide how to soak my whole body, as the pain kept me from diving in head first. I pulled the knife from my sock, scraping the blade across my wrist.

Nothing.

The side of the blade was too dull to do any damage. I bore the end into my wrist but couldn't break the skin. I saw scratches, but I didn't see blood.

I sat back on my feet, staring at the knife. I raised the point to my stomach, pressing against my sweatshirt. The pressure was evident on my stomach, but I lacked the strength to shove it through my skin.

I contemplated planting the knife in the sand, holding it in place, and falling on the blade. My body weight would cause the knife to penetrate my stomach. I dug a hole underneath the flowing water. Shoving the handle into the sand, I piled mud around it to keep the blade upright. The blade was sticking out of the water. I leaned down to hold the knife in place. I had one shot. I leaned back on the balls of my feet enough to stabilize the knife.

1...........2 3

I flung my torso toward the knife blade, falling face first into the freezing water. A piercing, horrible pain shot through my stomach and into my back. I was heaving in pain as soon as my body slammed against the ground. I picked myself up far enough to throw up the pizza I had eaten.

Seriously? After everything I have been through, I have to throw up just before I am going to die? What a sick joke.

The pain was so intense I couldn't hold myself above the water any longer. I fell into the water, unable to break the fall with my numb hands and arms. I coughed and gagged on the water as my face became submerged. I thought I might drown. I pulled up onto my elbows for air, and the movement exacerbated the pain in my stomach. I grasped a rock about a foot from where I had fallen, pulling my head toward it. Something was dragging underneath me. I placed my head sideways on the rock and felt under my stomach. My hand touched the handle of the knife. I wasn't sure if it was stuck inside of me. I couldn't take the pain of it anymore. I yanked it out, tossing it away from me.

I needed to calm down, so I concentrated on the water flowing downstream. My body began to feel numb. I was having a hard time moving my toes and hands. If I remained very still, the pain in my stomach seemed manageable. Now it was a waiting game. The damage was done.

Within minutes, I began experiencing bouts of heavy shivering. The movement of my body was uncontrollable. I thrashed forward into a fetal position, shaking violently. Each time, my head would fall off the rock and my mouth and nose would be covered in water. I gasped and gulped the creek water, trying not to drown.

I needed to flip onto my back to keep from gulping water. I didn't feel the pain in my stomach anymore, but the wound rendered me incapable of utilizing my stomach muscles. I turned my head in the opposite direction, pulling my arm through the underside of my body. I pushed both of my hands off the rocks and debris, forcing my body onto my back. My body splashed clumsily into the water like dead weight. The water soaked into my hair, covering the top of my head. I gasped in agony from pain. My forehead stung and pounded like a brain freeze. It took a couple minutes for my head and back to adjust to the cold water.

Lying on my back, I could see each breath in the cold as it floated toward the sky. I wondered how long it would take until I saw my last breath. Would I know it was my last breath? Would it hurt?

I wondered how big the knife wound was. It was impossible to sit up to inspect the damage, so I searched the sweatshirt with my fingers until I found a hole above my stomach in between my rib cage. I was afraid to feel the wound. I didn't want to feel the opening. I was relieved the self-injuring was over. I felt content if I changed my mind, I would be unable to leave. The wound would force a hypothermic suicide.

My focus now was on managing the shivering. My breath shortened seconds before every muscle contracted, thrusting me into a fetal position. The pain in my stomach made me want to scream, but all I could do was shake. I worried the movement was tearing the wound even more so I held onto my stomach while shivering, counting seconds until they ended.

The longer I lay in the creek, the shorter the bouts of shivering lasted and the longer time I had in between. I reasoned my body would eventually stop trying to warm itself. I figured the longer time between bouts, the closer I was to hyperthermia and death.

I lay as still as possible between shivering bouts. I didn't want the water to touch any part of my skin not already saturated. The still moments were peaceful. My body felt completely numb now. The pain was minimal. All was quiet around me. I longed for death, but the quietness and stillness were welcome. I could hear sounds of water lapping against the rocks and my body. I could hear my breathing. I hadn't been able to pause and just listen to anything other than my horrible thoughts for so long. The solace was comforting.

I felt I accomplished something big. For the first time in so many years, I had taken control. Nothing else could happen but death. And, this was the result of a decision I made, not one I had to grapple with anymore day in and day out. I had asserted dominance over my brain, finally. By dying, I would win. I had grown so tired of being dominated by the evil in my brain. I didn't have to live under the demands anymore. I didn't have to beat myself up anymore. Soon, I would no longer be in pain, in misery, or feeling guilt and shame. *I made this decision*. I was brave enough to take control. No one, not even God could take that decision away from me.

But, I couldn't deny the sadness.

My mind rested on my cousin John. I was desperate to see his face. I begged for his spirit to rescue me. While I finally felt in control, I also felt alone. I wanted him there with me. I didn't want to freeze to death alone in that creek. I wondered if God and John would have mercy on me for completing suicide. I hoped John had seen the amount of suffering I had endured, and would be anxiously waiting, holding my hand as I passed from body to spirit.

I thought of my family. Why didn't I leave a note? Because I didn't think I deserved to be mourned. Would they feel angry with me? Would they be happy I was dead? I hoped one day they would understand I was not someone they wanted in their life. I visualized daddy running across the yard, down the embankment, pulling me out of the creek, holding me in his arms and telling me it would be okay. But, I knew it could never be okay. I deserve to die. I am a horrible person and even in my last moment of pleading and bargaining, God has not found me worthy enough to save. How can I subject my family to me for the rest of their life? If I stay, they will eventually find out what a bad person I am. It is better for them if they never know the truth.

I thought of my friends at school. I pictured my roommate Allison and my friend Brad, wishing so badly I could have told them. I wished I had been brave and confident enough to explain death was the only option. I wished I knew they would still love me if they knew the truth about me. The thought of their rejection kept me silent, even though my rational side knew the worry was wrong. I knew they would love me anyway, but I was too scared to take the risk of losing them.

I thought of my cross-country team and all the fun times we had together on the road. I thought about Meredith, Avallina, and April. I wondered if they would be disappointed in me if they knew the coward I really was. I wished so badly I could travel back in time and revel in the times we had together. I wished I could relive them right now. We were like a family that had been through so much together. I wondered if I had told them, would they have understood and helped me? I wished they knew where I was now to come pull me out and tell me everything would be okay.

I sobbed at the thought of leaving all these people behind. How badly I didn't want it to end this way. How I wished I hadn't turned out to be the person I was. I wept loudly at what a disappointment I was to everyone and to God.

I screamed at the heavens.

"WHY?"

"WHY ME? WHAT DID I DO TO DESERVE THIS?"

As tears soaked my face, thoughts rested once again on my cousin, John. I had missed him so much since he died. I begged and begged him to come find me now. I wanted nothing other than to be with him. I wanted to see his face. I pleaded with God to make it end. I felt God at least owed me a quick death after everything He had put me through. I begged Him to send John to come and get me.

Why isn't death coming faster? How much longer do I have to wait? Haven't I suffered enough in twelve damn years? I want this to end!

I stared at the tall Georgia pines towering above me. Their treetops seem to stretch to the stars. The trunks and branches swayed slowly back and forth in the wind, and I could see hundreds of shining stars through them. In the water, I could see the yellow glow of the stars and moon glistening and reflecting as the motion of the water slowly trickled over my legs.

I pretended the pines were the gateway into Heaven. I envisioned their bold, beautiful branches swaying in the wind as a mourning dance for me as I lay dying at their strong roots. I envisioned my body drifting from life to death and their branches raising me up off the earth, passing me into the arms of my cousin. I closed my eyes and imagined John wrapping his arms around me, showing me the way into the stars. I envisioned the person I was on this earth disappearing forever. I imagined never feeling this pain again. I believed John would wrap me in light and love away from what I once was, placing me at the feet of a God who would forgive me for being that person. I hoped to learn the reason for all of the suffering. I had to believe everything I went through was not in vain. I hoped for some explanation. I needed to believe there was a smidgen of something good from it. I prayed the pain of stabbing myself and dying alone in this creek bed would, in the end, prove to be of some benefit to God. I knew there had been nothing beneficial about my life up to now for myself or anyone. There was only disappointment. All that was left was a hollow, horrible person.

A painful bout of shivering proved my fantasy was only imaginary as it thrashed me into reality. My body jolted forward in violent shivering and my visions escaped me. There is nothing here but darkness. No one is here. I am utterly alone. I am gravely injured, and unfortunately still alive. John is nowhere. There is no pathway to heaven lit for me to follow. I am freezing, alone, and suffering. Nothing has changed.

A dark fear entered my mind. I heard many times individuals who die by suicide go to Hell. The thought entered my mind, sending a surge of anger through my body. I wanted to remember the idiots who had the audacity to say such a stupid thing. I wanted to find them and tell them exactly what it feels like to believe there is no other way. I wanted to lecture them in a sermon at the pulpit on how it feels to be trapped in a life of servitude to a God who punishes and rewards in ways that breed suicidal behavior. I felt a fire light inside of me. I wanted to preach in my moment of death.

Regardless of how I viewed a higher being at that moment, I was not taught to believe God took pleasure in the suffering of others. I wasn't sure what I believed about God anymore, but I knew one thing for certain, He wouldn't be rejoicing in my lifeless body nearing death in this gruesome way. I had to believe if there was a God, He wouldn't cast demons in my direction. He would be lying beside me, freezing in the cold with me. He wouldn't stand over me like the preacher in the pulpit, chastising and condemning me. He would be holding my hand and wiping my tears. I refused to see God as an evil dictator rejoicing in my pain. I chose the God of empathy and compassion.

I had to believe there was something else. I had to believe there was another explanation. I needed to believe it was different than religion and conviction. *So if it isn't a hateful God, what could it be? Did this mean there is something behind this other than God? Is there another explanation? Have I been wrong about what God wants for me?*

All of a sudden, I felt confused. I didn't know what I believed and felt comfortable with having no urgency to define it. Maybe God really isn't an evil dictator in my mind. How can I find out for sure?

In that moment of uncertain thoughts and comforting anger, I knew I needed to escape death. Maybe it was the still, quiet of the night, helping me to find strength. Maybe it was the beauty of the pines and the mystery of the stars inspiring me not to give up. Or maybe John really was there with me. Maybe his spirit was sitting beside me begging and pleading with me to get up. Maybe *he* was lying beside me in this cold creek, holding my hand, and crying with me. Maybe John's spirit was the reason I decided to choose life no matter what life would look like after that night. Maybe it was John's spirit inspiring me to believe I had a life worth saving.

"SHIT! WHAT DO I DO NOW?" I screamed.

I sobbed at the thought of the pain I would experience getting up and out of the water.

NO! NO! NO! I have come this far, I cannot turn back now!

But, I had to. Something inside me wanted to live. I had made the decision. I needed to act, and act fast.

Now the focus was on living, no matter the cost.

I needed to save my life.

Chapter 20: Please Don't Shoot!

Saving my life proved harder than I imagined. My extremities were useless from the cold. My hands and feet were completely numb. It was going to be a race against time whether I survived or not. Instead of wishing for death to hurry, I was panicking to beat it.

I attempted to sit up, but my limbs and muscles couldn't cooperate. I used my wrists to push against the rocks with forced weight from my shoulders. My wrists slipped repeatedly from lack of feeling, causing me to splash back into the water. Each fall was painful and exhausting. I focused hard, making sure my wrists stayed in contact with the rocks. When I finally pushed far enough, I used the weight of my body to swing my leg over the top while pushing my other heel into the ground as hard as possible. I flopped onto my stomach screaming in agony as the cold water hit my chest and neck.

Get out of this water now, Chrissie!

My fingers couldn't move, so I shoved my fists into the mud pulling my body forward using my shoulders against the weight of the ground. I could move almost six inches this way. With every sliding movement over the ground, I bellowed at the intense ache reverberating through my stomach and back. I had no idea how deep the knife wound was, so was unaware of the damage caused by pulling it along the ground. But my wound wasn't a priority now. I needed to focus on getting help.

I finally managed to pull my body out of the water onto the sandy area bordering the creek and collapsed from exhaustion. The ground felt warm compared to the water. I looked at the embankment I needed to scale. Any other day, two steps were needed to hop over it, but tonight it looked like a mountain. I forgot I was partially frozen thinking I could just stand up and walk over it. I pushed away from the ground with my elbows to sit up. I pulled my legs underneath me preparing to stand. When the full weight of my body hit my quads, I collapsed face-first onto the ground. I spat out a mouthful of dirt and grit while panting heavily to breathe. My quads were completely fatigued from shivering and could bear no weight whatsoever.

With my legs out of commission, using elbows to crawl up the embankment was my only option. I dug both elbows into the dirt, shoving my weight onto them to get started. Using what little strength was left in my quads to pull my knees to my chest, I army-crawled on my elbows to gain any sort of distance. I felt like an inch worm, and could only gain about eighteen inches with this technique.

My head popped over the embankment after my third attempt. I felt completely depleted of energy. There was no way I could make it back to daddy's house at this pace, especially on concrete. *Where can I go for help?* I looked across the large yard and saw a porch-light. That was it. I needed to get to the light. *No matter what happens, do not stop focusing on the light.*

The yard wasn't too big, but knowing I couldn't walk made it seem like miles. I pushed hard on my elbows, swung my leg over the embankment, and rolled onto my back in the grass. I looked at the stars, completely different now than from the creek. I looked down at the creek where I was laying only minutes earlier. *I can change my mind right now and roll back into the water if I want.* I scanned the water for the knife, but couldn't see anything in the dark. I looked at the pines dancing in the wind. *You made the decision to live. Don't turn back. You'll figure out what to do later, but now you need to get help.* I took a deep breath, turned away from the pines, and promised myself I wouldn't look back no matter what.

Swinging my leg over, I rolled onto the grass. I pulled my legs underneath me again believing it would be easier to stand on flat ground and positioned my body to sit on my heels. I counted to three, lunged forward to stand, and felt the painful reminder of my quad fatigue. Because my hands couldn't work, I broke my fall in the grass with my face. It hurt like hell, but I noticed I could get farther quicker by doing this, rather than inching forward on my elbows. So, I pulled myself with my elbows doing again just as before. This time, I pulled up my body, taking a very large step while bracing to fall on my shoulder. Gaining so much more ground this way, I did this over and over, crashing my body onto the ground each time. It hurt badly, but I could get to the light in half the time it would take dragging my body with my elbows.

Finally, I was only a few feet from the driveway. I couldn't fall head first into concrete, so I dug my fingernails and hands deep into the dirt pulling myself forward inch by inch until my right hand slammed into the concrete. I pulled myself over the concrete with my elbows until I reached a parked car in the garage. I used the car to offset my muscle weakness balancing between leaning onto the car and pulling my legs. Reaching inside door of the covered garage, I pulled myself up the stairs by hanging onto the banister. I banged on the door screaming for help. There was a white, embroidered, country curtain blocking my view into the house. I squinted, pushing my head closer to the glass to see inside when I realized I was staring down the barrel of a handgun.

"DON'T SHOOT ME! OH GOD, PLEASE DON'T SHOOT ME! I NEED HELP!" I shouted at the door.

The curtain hurriedly pushed aside, and my desperate eyes locked with a frightened older gentleman's. He calmed down upon hearing my pleas for help, put down the gun, and opened the door. A frightened woman peeked around the corner. Her face showed how terrifying I must have looked. The man grabbed me around the waist as I stumbled through the doorway, guiding me to a stool his wife had put in the middle of the kitchen before she disappeared. The man was shaking and shouting at me asking for information. I couldn't look him in the face. I just kept repeating:

"Call the Methodist minister, Jay Hodges. Call the Methodist minister, Jay Hodges. Call the Methodist minister, Jay Hodges..."

Hands shaking, the man grabbed the phone while sifting through the phone book looking for my dad. I closed my eyes, fighting the urge to crawl back into the creek and die. I was so embarrassed. Just as I thought about getting up to leave, a warm, yellow blanket was wrapped around my back and tightened around my chest like a cocoon. I opened my eyes to the wife tucking the blanket in itself so it would stay wrapped. She was standing in front of me with desperate, inquisitive eyes. With no energy to explain, I closed my eyes again, tucking my chin to my chest. I had no words to comfort her.

The man was stumbling over his words asking the receiving end if he was speaking to the Methodist minister, Jay Hodges. The man could barely get a word in edge-wise until he recited his physical address. Then there was silence.

The room was tense and awkward, but I didn't care. I knew these poor people needed answers, but I didn't want to speak. They stole helpless looks at one another, while I stared at the floor. I mumbled under my breath how I had failed, wishing I had stayed in the creek. I dreaded seeing daddy. It was too late to go back now since he knew. *How did I end up here? The plan to die was working. Why didn't I stick with it?*

All of the reasons for crawling out of the creek bed were nowhere to be found. They disappeared somewhere between the pine trees and this house. Nothing was going to be different. Nothing would be okay. I was still the same disgusting, shameful girl I was before. But now it was worse because my family would know the truth. I was a disgrace. I could not even succeed at killing myself. I was worthless. And now I had to face it. This was worse than dying.

Screeching tires and a familiar truck engine shattered the silence. I heard the truck door slam and in a half second, daddy was beating on the back door. I braced myself. The door flung open and daddy's eyes pierced straight through me. Unable to look him in the face, I stared at the floor and started sobbing. He wasted no time telling me to get my tail up and into the truck. I pulled the warm, yellow blanket off, looking thankfully and apologetically at the woman. She stared back at me with confused tears in her eyes.

I pushed off the stool, falling forward onto the floor into a pool of blood. As my body warmed up, the wound in my stomach began bleeding. I yelped from the pain. I couldn't stand up or walk. In a swift movement, daddy swept me in his arms, bolting out the door.

I left wondering if those wonderful individuals would ever fully grasp the kindness they displayed. I wondered if they would ever forgive me for putting them in that position. They felt helpless and I couldn't provide them with the comfort or answers they needed.

Daddy threw me in the passenger side of the truck, slamming the door. I watched him frantically run around the front of the vehicle toward the driver's side. I knew he was angry.

This is it. I have to say it out loud.

I closed my eyes. *Will he understand? Will he believe me?*

The tires screeched out of the driveway so aggressively it frightened me. I could understand his fear and confusion, but I was afraid to talk to him when he was this angry. We drove in circles around the block as he asked me questions. I stayed quiet. He began reprimanding me for how irresponsible it was to run alone in the dark. I pulled back, realizing how misled he was about tonight.

I felt defensive. "I wasn't on a run! I didn't get attacked! No one did this to me. I did this to myself. I tried to kill myself."

I saw the light-bulb go on in his head just before it exploded. His fear and anger were palpable.

"Chrissie, you better start explaining yourself, right now. You better start telling me what this is about."

The moment I had avoided for twelve years was here. I had to admit these stupid and ridiculous thoughts. I promised myself I would protect everyone from this, and now I had to break that promise because I failed at suicide. My brain warned me about saying these things out loud. *What would happen afterward?* I was so terrified.

My mouth opened, but the words weren't there. I started crying. How could I articulate twelve years of suffering? I realized the truck was stopped. Parked in the middle of our street, daddy wasn't moving until he got answers. I was trapped. I couldn't escape this situation until I told the truth.

"I wanted to kill myself. I wanted to die. I don't want to live anymore because since I was eight years old, all I've worried about is whether or not I am going to throw up or whether or not I am supposed to be gay. I have no idea if these two things are related, but every time I worry about them, I get the same feeling in the back of my neck, my chest, and my arms. It doesn't make sense. I don't understand it. But, I am tired of living with it. I didn't know what else to do. The only way I knew to stop it was to kill myself."

I waited for a response. I would have taken any response. But, I got none. There was silence. I dropped my chin down, continuing to cry. I knew he probably hated me now.

Daddy forcefully put the truck into drive and said, "Chrissie, I have no idea what you are talking about or what is going on with you. But, one thing I do know is your life is going to change from this moment on. I don't know how, but things will never be the same as they were for you ever again."

I believed he was talking out of fear, so those were the words he needed to hear himself. Maybe he was saying those words to make sense out of it all. Maybe he really believed what he said. Maybe he thought I was crazy. I didn't know. But, I chose to believe in his statement that somehow he wanted me to hear no matter what, he would still love me. I decided to hold on like hell to that belief.

Right now, it was all I had.

Chapter 21: Why Am I Still Alive?

Daddy's truck came to a screeching halt in the driveway. He carried me into the house and put me in the bathtub instructing me to take off my muddied clothes and run a warm bath. Why wasn't he being compassionate at all? He was coarse and distant. Didn't he realize how much suffering I had been through all these years? This confirmed the fear that if people knew who I really was, they would be disappointed.

Sobbing, I peeled off my muddy, blood-soaked sweatpants and threw them on the floor. I was scared to take off the sweatshirt unveiling my damaged stomach. I didn't want to know what I was capable of. I pulled off the shirt and leaned forward so I didn't have to look. The clear water gushing out of the faucet quickly turned a cloudy dark red color as it hit the bathtub. Warming up was incredibly painful. My toes, feet, and legs felt as if they were going to explode through my skin which itched so badly, it hurt to be touched. The pain was excruciating. Also, the warmer I became, the more painful my stomach became. I leaned back to look at my wound. I had over an inch slab of skin cut away from my stomach. It was gaping open and blood was seeping into the water.

I watched the dark reddish-brown water cover my knees. Linda suddenly appeared beside the tub. I turned away from her. I didn't want to explain it again. I only mumbled about being sorry. We sat in silence.

I could hear daddy talking loudly on the phone. *What was going to happen now?* I couldn't sit in this mud bath any longer it was so painful, so I unplugged the drain. The feeling in my feet, calves, and quads was returning, so I pulled myself up to sit on the side of the tub. Linda wrapped me in a towel and helped me to my room. *How did I end up back here?* I was supposed to be dead.

We sat on the edge of the bed as she helped me put on clothes. Every movement was painful. I started to explain to Linda what happened, but realized I didn't have the energy. I stopped talking and we sat in silence.

Daddy rushed into the room. It was time to go. He carried me to the truck. The cab was blazing hot. The heat wasn't helping my pain level, but I was scared to say anything to daddy. I figured I had put him through enough. Neither of us spoke about what happened or where we were going. We pulled up to an emergency room in downtown Atlanta. Daddy set me in a waiting room chair while he checked me in with staff. I was miserably uncomfortable. I felt angry. *Why am I here? Why didn't I just stay in the creek? I would be dead by now if I had stayed. Because I am weak and couldn't go through with the suicide, I have to tell these hospital employees what happened. They are going to judge me and think I am worthless.*

I wanted to be treated with disdain to prove I didn't deserve to be alive. I wanted to see on anyone's face I was the lowest piece of shit on the planet. I wanted to see people look at me in disgust. I wanted to see in other people's reactions the lowlife I was so I would get through this and make sure I died next time. I knew everyone was going to judge me anyway, so I hoped they wouldn't hide it from me.

Daddy came back with a clipboard of paperwork. He took a deep breath and began filling it out. I felt ashamed. I cringed as he checked the self-inflicted box. *What kind of a daughter am I? He is probably so embarrassed about having someone like me as his daughter. I wouldn't blame him if he just dropped me off and never looked back. What a disappointment I must be to him.*

Daddy dropped off the paperwork with the receptionist who probably read the 'self-inflicted' box and judged me. Shortly after, a nurse called my name. Daddy carried me to the private ER room. He laid me on the examining table and sat in the corner. There was nothing left to say. The pain in my stomach was so agonizing, I could barely stand it. Almost immediately a tall, handsome doctor walked in. His cologne filled the room. I was mortified to tell this gorgeous doctor what I had done. He asked a series of questions, and I answered them like a robot never making eye contact with him. He probably thought I was an ungrateful piece of human crap. I explained my thoughts and actions over the last twelve years in the most sarcastic tone possible. I knew he probably didn't care. I didn't care either. I just wanted to do what needed to be done so I could get out of there and succeed at suicide next time.

The doctor examined my stomach and repeated back to me the ridiculous story I had just told him. It sounded so irrational and stupid when I heard someone else tell it. I could hardly believe it was the story of my life. I looked at the wall as I nodded, wiping away the tears. There was a long, silent pause before I felt his hand gently rest on mine. I didn't move. I was too ashamed to look him in the face.

His words pierced the silence, "Chrissie, I am so sorry for what you have been through. It must have been so horrible for you. I am so glad you are alive. We are going to do everything we can to make sure you are okay, I promise."

I looked up at him, tears streaming down my cheeks. His gaze was tender and sincere. I was dumbfounded. This man knows nothing but the bad parts about me, yet he believes my experience is real and believes there is hope. I looked at daddy. He was sitting in the corner with his head in his hands. I wondered if he would ever feel as confident in me as this doctor did. I hoped he would. I looked in the doctor's sincere eyes and said, "Thank you, Doctor. Thank you for believing me."

The doctor worried I might have punctured an internal organ and wanted to perform exploratory surgery. I was happy to be given anesthesia because I could barely stand the pain anymore. Surgery would happen within an hour.

Mama arrived shortly after meeting with the doctor. She was confused and upset. She came into the room, bombarding me with questions. My pain level was too intense to engage in conversation. Before the nurses came to take me into surgery she asked with concern, "I just have to ask you, do you really think you are gay?"

I was startled into disbelief. Every ounce of hope I had gathered after seeing the doctor was shattered. Did she not believe what I told her happened? Does she not see this had been a worry I couldn't control? A hot wave of anger consumed me. I felt it in my toes as it moved into my stomach before hitting my face and my head.

What in the hell did she just say to me? Why the hell would I be here now if coming out of the closet was the solution? Am I gay? If I were really gay, I would be GAY...I wouldn't be worrying day in and day out whether or not I'm SUPPOSED to be?

I couldn't respond, fearing how badly I might unleash on her. How dare she ask that question after everything I had just been through? I wish the answer was that simple. And furthermore, would it matter if I was? I had just attempted suicide. If I were actually gay, wouldn't my longing to be dead because of that be the real issue?

A second before I opened my mouth to spew venom, the door flew open and the nurse told me it was time to go. "Thank goodness," I thought.

My mom's question triggered the bad thoughts and feelings. *What if, instead of facing whether or not you are supposed to be gay, you decided you should just die? What if you did all of this for nothing just to cover up the fact that you will have to date women one day? What if you are just in denial and you really want to be gay, but you just don't want to admit it?*

I couldn't take it. How could I seriously be debating this right after I shoved a knife in my stomach? I started to cry. The fluorescent lights whisked above me as I was wheeled into surgery. *Why are they going to fix my stomach? I don't deserve to live. Why didn't I stay in the creek? This would have all been over by now if I had. Worrying now proves it will never end. I said the fears out loud and the worry is still there, doesn't that prove it is real? Wouldn't telling someone prove one way or another?*

I didn't realize how hard I was crying until I felt a hand on the side of my face. The nurse was wiping away my tears. I mumbled how sorry I was about being such a horrible person. She put her hand on my forehead, looked in my eyes and said, "Chrissie, everything is going to work out. I need you to trust me. I promise you will be okay. Please believe me."

I squeezed my eyes shut and tears rolled onto her hand. I held as tightly as I could to the hope she was giving me. My doctor and this nurse knew nothing about me except my irrational fears and suicide attempt, yet they still had compassion and empathy. I wanted nothing more than to believe them. If two strangers didn't think I was a disgusting and disgraceful monster, maybe other people would accept me too.

I nodded my head and she smiled at me. My reality began to slow down as the double doors swung open. My doctor was waiting with sterilized gloves ready to perform surgery. My eyes held open long enough to watch him smile and nod at me before I drifted into sleep.

Chapter 22: I'm Mentally Ill Now, so My Opinions Don't Matter

I awoke to my arm being forcefully jerked. "Ouch!" I yelled, opening my eyes to see a red headed nurse. She sneered at me while attempting to wrap a blood pressure cuff around my bicep. I groaned, trying to pull my arm away. A horrendous pain shot through my torso as my stomach muscles turned to fire, and I yelped loudly.

"You need to cooperate and this will go quicker," she snapped.

"Lady, I'm in pain here. Can you be nicer?"

Ignoring me, she continued to yank my arm. I turned my head away from her before saying something I would probably regret.

Bitch. I hope she goes off duty soon.

She finally left. I tried rolling on my side, but was prevented by a horrendous pain in my stomach. Tracing the middle of my torso with my fingertips outside my hospital gown, I felt a line of staples about eight inches long. It was too dark and I was too exhausted to figure out how to turn on a light. My eyes closed and I imagined I was anywhere but in that hospital bed.

I was yanked out of sleep again by someone pulling at my arm, annoying me. *What the hell, can't these jerks let me sleep?* I mumbled something under my breath before facing a different nurse. She looked at me nervously, apologizing for waking me. She said it was necessary to check vitals every few hours. My face softened, and I thanked her. She wrote in a chart and excused herself from the room.

Turning my head toward the window, I was shocked to find my Aunt Carol sitting next to the bed. I panicked. *What is she doing here?*

How could daddy let her be here? Does she know what happened? Why would they tell her?

Our eyes met in awkward silence. I thanked her for being there and turned my head away, pretending to fall asleep. I was pissed. *Why did my family call her? I don't want anyone to know about this. Did they tell her what happened? Does she know about the bad thoughts?* I felt vulnerable, sad, and angry with my family. They had no right to disclose these details to anyone.

Why didn't I just stay in the creek? I could be dead now. Why in the hell did I get up? I am weak and a failure. That was my chance and I blew it. It could all be over now, but I was weak and chickened out.

I didn't want to cry in front of Aunt Carol. Closing my eyes I focused on my breathing, and thankfully sleep took over.

I awoke to the warmth of the sun on my cheeks. It was morning and I opened my eyes to find daddy sitting beside me reading a book. I stirred a little, catching his attention. He asked how I felt, and I shook my head. How do I even begin to answer that question? He filled me in on the details of my surgery. I had successful exploratory surgery to make sure no internal organs were damaged and apparently I was lucky.

"What happens now?" I asked.

"In a couple days, you will be transferred to an inpatient psychiatric facility."

My head jerked back. *What is a psychiatric facility? Is that like a mental home?*

"Umm, why am I going to a psych ward?" I asked.

"Chrissie, you just attempted suicide and we need to figure out what is wrong. This is a good place to start."

The room began to spin. *Will I be placed in a straight-jacket and shackles?* Panic began to overtake me, but the pain in my stomach wouldn't let me move. My neck began tingling and my arms started going numb. I felt I couldn't breathe. I started to cry, but my stomach hurt so badly I stopped. I was angry at my dad. *Does he hate me so much he will just drop me off at a mental hospital so he doesn't have to deal with me? I was right all along. If my family knew all of this about me, they would be embarrassed and ashamed. How easy it must be for them to just drop me off at a mental institution and forget all about me.*

"HOW LONG WILL I BE THERE? WHAT IS GOING TO HAPPEN TO ME? WHEN WILL I GET TO COME HOME?" I demanded.

"Chrissie, you need to calm down. This is temporary until we figure out what to do next."

Calm down? How in the hell am I supposed to calm down? Why can't we figure this out at home? Why can't we forget this happened? I want to go back to school! I want to see my friends! I want to go back to everything before this happened! WHY DID I EVER GET OUT OF THE CREEK? I WILL FOREVER BE DEEMED SOME CRAZY PSYCHO WHO TRIED TO KILL HERSELF!

Daddy recognized what was happening and stood up. "Why don't we get you up and moving around? Let's take a walk down the hall."

I needed to get some air, so I agreed. Daddy raised the head of the bed so I was sitting up. I tried to move my right leg toward the side of the bed, and groaned in pain. My quad muscles were so sore I could barely flex them. Daddy pulled my legs over the side as I pushed off the head of the bed with my arms to propel myself forward. I didn't realize how pertinent stomach muscles are in movement until experiencing the inability to use them. Daddy gave me the rolling IV to balance. My toes barely touched the ground. Pushing with my arms, I scooted to the edge of the bed, shifting my weight onto my feet. The weight was too much to bear on my quads that were so sore. Daddy pulled me onto my feet and held me until I found the right weight balance. The staples wouldn't allow me to stand up straight. I took one step and my head started spinning.

"I'm going to throw up...oh God...please don't let me throw up...what if I throw up...oh no, help me!'" I yelled. The bad feelings started. I felt I was going to throw up and couldn't move or escape. Daddy lowered me back onto the bed.

My life is over. I cannot even walk. I'm going to spend the rest of my life in a mental home. I'm going to throw up and it's going to hurt my stomach so bad. Please don't let me throw up. God, PLEASE don't let me throw up.

"Let's try again, and just go really slow," Daddy said. I was terrified I would throw up. The panic was overwhelming. I stood up slowly. Daddy was on one side and I held the IV on the other. I took one slow step at a time, barely moving forward. Every movement blasted my stomach and legs with pain. We walked outside the room and started down the hall. Daddy was talking about normal life things, but I wasn't listening. I was watching the patients, nurses, and workers. *Did they know how lucky they are? They can live their lives without worrying about all the bullshit I have to worry about. They get to go home tonight and sleep in their beds. I will be sleeping in the nut-house.* I wished I could be any one of those people around me other than myself. I failed at suicide and would now have to live in a mental hospital. My life was over.

My anxiety and panic about throwing up began to overwhelm me again. I told daddy we needed to turn around. Turning slowly, we crept back to my room. As long as I didn't make any sudden movements, I felt in control of the throw up feelings. I was relieved to turn the corner to my room. All I wanted was to go to sleep and never wake up. I was living in a nightmare.

Daddy said my hair needed to be washed. I felt the top of my head and found globs of mud stuck to my scalp. Daddy scooted a chair into the bathroom and helped me sit down close enough to lean my head into the sink. He stood over me, washing off all the dirt and mud carefully so as not to yank on my hair. *Why does he want to do something so nice for me? Doesn't he hate me now? I am a horrible person and a disappointing daughter. I can't imagine how he can even look at me after what happened.*

I felt guilty. I was ashamed. I wanted to apologize. I wanted to tell him how sorry I was he ended up with a daughter like me. He deserved so much better. He was such a good person, and he had to live with the embarrassment of having me as a daughter.

I assumed he was biding his time, knowing he'd never have to deal with me again once I was in the mental hospital. I wanted to believe there was a possibility he would love me again or be proud of me. I wanted to believe he could understand what was happening to me wasn't the life I wanted. This wasn't the person I wanted to be. But, that was impossible. All I felt was shame and embarrassment. Maybe it would be best for everyone if I just disappeared into the hospital, completely forgotten.

I fell asleep quickly after the short walk down the hall. I woke again the next morning to the sun on my face. Mama was pulling back the curtains, and my doctor was in the room. It was the first time I had seen him since the bad night. I felt embarrassed. He walked over to me, smiled, and asked how I was doing.

"As good as to be expected, I guess," I said shyly.

He examined my stomach, giving a timeline of how it would heal. The staples would be removed in a few weeks. I wondered if they would let me out of the psych ward to return to the hospital. I didn't dare ask. He told me a psychiatrist would be stopping by to have a session with me. I immediately felt defensive and angry. *I don't want to see a psychiatrist. I don't want to talk to anyone about what happened. Why isn't anyone asking me what I want? Everyone is making decisions for me without asking for my input. This is still my life, dammit! Why doesn't my opinion matter? Is it because I'm crazy and mentally unstable now?* I felt small, incompetent, and insignificant.

He left and I ignored everyone in the room. The tension was palpable. If I dared state my opinion, I might have exploded into words of hatred and anger. So, I remained quiet and cooperative against my will.

I didn't want to retell and relive everything about the suicide attempt to a stranger. Saying everything out loud made me feel worse, and I already felt horrible enough. No one was respecting my wishes and privacy. *Why do I feel I am being punished? No one is asking me what I want. They are just making decisions for me without caring how I feel.*

A little while later, there was a knock. Daddy opened the door and in walked a doctor accompanied by four younger individuals carrying clipboards. He introduced himself as a psychiatrist while the other four introduced themselves as 'interns'.

What the hell? What are these students doing here? This is bullshit. They look my age! I don't have to talk to anyone about my situation and my life. I want nothing to do with these people. What do I look like, a test study? I'm not a lab rat! They can go to Hell. I didn't ask for this, so I don't have to participate.

The psychiatrist asked what happened. I barely responded with anything other than simple facts. "I attempted suicide, now I'm here." I wasn't going to put my life on display for these idiots. He seemed agitated at my response, but I didn't care. When I decided to answer any of his questions, I responded sardonically and sarcastically. I was mortified an actual psychiatrist would subject me to talking in front of these people about such a private, traumatic event, while they scribbled on their clipboards. *What kind of professional is this jerk? They are probably judging me, condemning me, and taking pity on me.* I became so angry at their note-taking I stopped talking altogether, just staring at them with disdain and disgust.

The less I talked, the more patronizing and condescending the psychiatrist's tone and questions became. He talked to me as if I was in preschool and kept asking me to 'cooperate', as if I was a criminal ready to be prosecuted. I was seething with anger. *Stop asking me questions like I am an idiot. Stop talking to me like I'm an idiot.*

I told the psychiatrist I was done talking, turning my head toward the window. After a few awkward moments, the psychiatrist and his entourage left. As soon as they left, I began crying uncontrollably. I was humiliated. It was hard enough for me to tell my family, but to be put on display this way made me feel like the scum of the earth. *Wouldn't a psychiatrist have more tact or compassion?* I was at a new low with shame and guilt.

Later in the evening, my doctor stopped by. He explained I was to be released in the morning. I was allowed to ride with my parents to the inpatient psychiatric hospital if I wished. My stay at the hospital depended on how well I responded to treatment.

What the hell is 'treatment'? How am I supposed to respond? How do they treat a 'horrible person' that cannot figure out whether or not she's going to throw up or turn gay? This makes no sense.

I decided when I got to the mental hospital, I would agree with everything anyone said to me. I wanted nothing but to be out of the mental hospital, and I wasn't even there yet. I would do whatever they wanted me to so I could get out. *After I'm released, I'll pretend I am cured and will find a truly successful way to kill myself with no mistakes or changing my mind. I was so stupid to give up in the creek, and I won't make that mistake again. Next time I will do it right and I won't survive. I was a fool to give up before.*

I promised myself next time I would not survive. This gave me hope to tolerate and endure the psychiatric hospitalization.

Chapter 23: I am NOT One of These Crazy People!

The psychiatric facility was in the middle of nowhere. From the outside it didn't look like the scary mental homes in horror movies, which was somewhat comforting. I didn't see any wheelchairs with cobwebs in random places or barefoot people with wild hair trying to scale the walls. I hoped it would be the same inside.

Daddy was already waiting for us when mama and I arrived. My quads were still so sore it was excruciatingly painful to walk to the admissions room. I could barely walk faster than a turtles pace. Hunched over because of the staples in my stomach, I held onto furniture and railings to keep the weight off my legs, looking like a crazy person as I walked through the admissions office. I plopped in a chair in front of the administrator. The short walk from the car had exhausted all my energy. She asked me to tell her what happened. I rolled my eyes.

Seriously? How many times do I have to tell this damn story? It becomes more humiliating every time I tell it.

She looked at me quizzically, asking me why I rolled my eyes.

"Because I'm sick of telling the story about what a horrible person I am. Killing myself is the only option because it will never go away."

She raised her eyebrows, reassuring me I would not have to tell everyone here my story if I didn't want to. However by telling her, she would make certain I was placed with the right psychologist to help me figure out a plan.

What is a plan? A plan for what? This is a joke. There was no way around it, so I proceeded to tell her how everything changed for me in elementary school when Jeff threw up in my classroom. I was as detailed as I could be in the least hopeful and annoying tone. I wanted her to hear how horrible I was so she would understand and agree that I should be dead. I was sick of putting my disgusting life on display for everybody for no reason. *No one can do anything to help me. There is no hope. So I am going to be an asshole to anyone who forces me to talk about it from now on.*

She listened intently. I noticed my parents were also engaged in the story as well. I guess I had been pretty vague with them since the suicide attempt because of the shame and guilt. After I wrapped up with how I ended up there, I stopped talking and looked at the floor. I was waiting to hear the worst. I was waiting to hear her say I was a horrible, despicable individual who was weak, couldn't control her mind, and needed to be locked up for life.

She took her time responding, which made the bad feelings begin in my neck and arms. I started to feel I couldn't breathe and needed to get out of there, when she finally broke the silence.

"What you have experienced sounds familiar, but I cannot put my finger on it right now. I think we will be able to help you feel better, and I know exactly which psychologist to pair you with."

She was incredibly thoughtful and sincere. I did not expect that.

I allowed myself to feel a spark of hope when I heard her say it sounded familiar. *What did familiar mean? Does this mean there are other people like me? Does this mean there is some kind of help for the thoughts?*

"In the meantime, I need to make sure you are taking the medication we give you every day. This is important because it will give you relief from the depression."

Depression? What depression? This has nothing to do with depression. Why would she believe I was a depressed person? Have my parents told her things I don't know? Do they think I am depressed?

This is bullshit. Now they are going to treat me like some crazy person. I'm not like 'depressed' people. I have friends, I am outgoing, and I have a life. I don't wallow in self-pity and misery like depressed people do. I was furious, snapping back to the state of mind of doing whatever they said just to get out of this place. I chose not to openly acknowledge her misled depression comment.

She introduced us to a hospital worker who showed me to my room. It took several keys to get inside my new home. We walked into a big open room called the 'milieu'. Reality hit me hard when I saw the thick, plated glass. I was a mental patient in a mental hospital. I was like a crazed, caged animal in this awful place. There was a nurses' station for dispensing meds, a gathering room with a TV, horrible dirty couches, and the ugliest excuse for a Christmas tree I had ever seen. *Will I live here forever? Will I ever get out of here? How long will I have to stay here?* Tears began welling up.

I do not belong here! How can my parents leave me here? Do they hate me so much they will just leave me here forever? I don't deserve to be here, I am not like all of these other crazy people in here!

The bad feelings started in my hands and arms. I couldn't catch my breath and began sweating as the worker ushered us into my new room. My parents and I waited in silence. I couldn't look them in the face. *How in the hell can they do this to me? I hate them. How easy it must be for them to dump me here. Their embarrassing daughter can live her life in a crazy house with the crazy nut jobs so they don't have to deal with her anymore. I knew this would happen. I should have stayed in the creek.*

A nurse walked in, interrupting my thoughts. She was going over schedules, rules, and group meetings, but all I heard was "blah, blah, blah." I wasn't listening to her. I didn't care. I wanted to crawl under that ugly, nasty blanket on the twin bed and disappear. She sliced through my thoughts when she asked me to hand over my bag.

"No," I replied.

"Yes, Chrissie. We have to make sure there is nothing in your bag that can be used to harm yourself."

Oh my God, this is a nightmare.

I shoved my bag at her and went to lie down on the gross, ugly bed. *This is ridiculous. How did I end up here? I don't belong in this stupid locked ward. Who do they think I am?* I didn't bother watching the nurse search my bag, because it would only piss me off more. She placed what was left on the dresser, excusing herself so we could say goodbye.

I barely spoke to my parents before they left. They said goodbye, telling me they would visit soon, but I didn't lift my head. The nurse pushed the door open when my parents left, which annoyed me. I got up to shut it, but she stopped me, telling me I was not allowed to close the door completely because I was on suicide watch.

This is bullshit! All I want is some privacy. I am not a freaking criminal. Why am I being punished?

I gave her an angry look and shook my head.

"Whatever," I responded.

It was noisy outside my room. I squeezed the pillow over my ears. I didn't want to hear those crazy people screaming obscenities, or talking about feces, or whatever they probably do in this place.

A knock on the door startled me, and I heard a girl's voice saying, "Hello."

I lifted the pillow just enough to see the face of a heavy set, shorter girl with wild looking hair, peeking her head around the doorway. We made eye contact, and she came into my room without asking if it was okay.

"What do you want?" I asked bluntly.

"Hi there, I just wanted to say hello and welcome. We just got out of group and are heading to the cafeteria. We will be watching TV afterward if you want to join us. What's your name?"

"No. I'm not hungry and I don't want to watch TV," I replied, turning my head back underneath the pillow.

She lingered like she wanted to say something else before she shuffled out the door. I couldn't believe I had been so rude to someone I didn't know. That wasn't like me. But, I didn't care. She was probably some freaky, crazy person. I didn't want any of these people to think I was one of them. I was nothing like them. They needed to know I was not a mentally insane person.

I dozed off only to be woken by a loud, annoying knock at my door. I bolted up, yelping at the pain in my stomach. The nurse came in telling me it was time to eat. I was holding my stomach and gasping in pain.

"I'm not hungry. I'm too tired and in too much pain to move."

She reluctantly said she would bring food to me just once since I was still recovering from surgery, but I shouldn't get used to it.

"Gee, thanks," I said sarcastically, rolling my eyes then putting the pillow back over my head.

I could hear all the crazy people filing past my room going to dinner. I peeked through the covers to see what they looked like. I imagined everyone was probably drooling or shouting curse words. I knew eventually I'd have to pretend to get along with them, but for now I was going to do anything necessary to avoid them. Could I avoid talking to anyone and still get out quickly? To my surprise, I didn't see anyone looking over the top crazy. I guessed once I spent time with them though, that would change.

The nurse annoyingly barged in with a tray of food without asking if she could enter. I was starving but didn't want her to know. I asked her to put it on the nightstand. She slammed the tray down, hesitated, and scurried out.

I waited several minutes, making sure she was gone before I pulled myself up. I didn't want anyone to know I lied about being hungry. The food didn't look too bad. I expected to see cockroaches and maggots crawling in the mashed potatoes. I ate a bite of chicken, and then began shoveling food Into my mouth as fast as I could. A spoonful of rice went down the wrong pipe. I breathed in, unable to get air. I tried coughing and my stomach exploded with pain. I was choking on a damn piece of rice! I couldn't cough, breathe, or move because of the staples and incision in my stomach. I slammed my hand down on the nurse's button, and as I bent over coughing through the pain, the rice flew out of my mouth onto the bed.

The Invisible Side of Obsessive-Compulsive Disorder

A different nurse ran through the door with a panicked look. As soon as our eyes met, I began crying. She was by my side in a flash. I couldn't get any words out, I was sobbing so uncontrollably.

"I'm so sorry. I'm miserable. I didn't want to end up here. I hate myself. I hate my life. I'm so scared it will never get better!" I cried to her.

The nurse sat beside me listening as I rattled my apologies. Then, the only noise filling my room was my sobbing. After a couple minutes, she took the tray off of my lap, pulled the covers up to my chin, and put her hand on my shoulder.

"You will be okay," she said. "Just give it time. It's not as bad here as you think it is. We are here to help you through this. If you give it a chance, you may be surprised."

She stood up, turned off the light, and quietly left. *How am I going to survive this place? I am alone and hopeless. My family abandoned me here. Everything I believed about saying the thoughts out loud has come true. My brain always told me if I said the fears out loud everyone would hate me and I'd be deemed 'crazy'. And, here I am. I am alone in a mental institution with people who care nothing about me.*

My first night in the psychiatric ward was as miserable as I expected. I cried myself to sleep. I was lonelier than I had ever felt in my life.

Chapter 24: You Don't Know What It Is Like to be ME.

For several days, I avoided talking to staff and patients. I was 'too tired' to attend group sessions. I dodged going to the cafeteria by complaining about the pain in my stomach. I spent as much time alone and under the covers as possible.

When I did emerge from my room, I was surprised to see the patients seemed like actual humans. I didn't notice any violent, drooling, or potentially homicidal acting individuals. But, I figured it was only a matter of time until I did. I looked at the floor when passing anyone in the hall and ignored their attempts at saying "hello" or "how are you feeling?" Every day, I took my medication and returned to my room.

Day Four, the nurse who was there when I almost choked informed me of an appointment with my psychologist. I didn't move or speak. She walked over and sat in the chair beside the bed.

"Just so you know, if you are not participating in group sessions or therapy, you will stay here longer," she said.

I looked at her with wide, angry eyes. "What? Why the hell does it matter if I go to group sessions? Those have nothing to do with me. Nothing in those groups is going to help me. You people have no idea what it is like to be me and to live in this misery every damn day!"

"You will never know if you don't try. You might be surprised if you give a little effort. If you want to get out of here, you need to start participating. Your therapy session is in ten minutes."

I was irritated, sick of her saying 'I might be surprised'. *She doesn't know anything about me! I don't need a pep talk from a clueless nurse who gets to leave this place of hell every night. It's easy for her to be so positive, she isn't locked in!*

So, basically I have to pretend to like the people here. I have to pretend these clinicians give a damn about me. I have to pretend I'm better in order to get back into the real world. God, I am so sick of pretending. My bad thoughts and feelings kept me imprisoned for twelve years, now I am physically living in a prison for saying them out loud!

Begrudgingly, I pulled myself up to 'make the effort'. Information about my appointment was taped to the door. I grabbed the sheet and started walking down the hall. As I passed the TV room, I caught the eye of an African-American man with glasses. He smiled and waved at me. I paused, staring back at him. There was something genuine about his gesture. I furrowed my brow, half-smiled back at him, and quickly shuffled toward the psychologist's office.

I hobbled into the office, plopping down in a chair across from a bearded man wearing glasses. He seemed happy to see me, but I didn't return the enthusiasm. He started with small talk about his position. I heard, "blah, blah, blah." When he asked me to tell him my story from beginning to end, I rolled my eyes and grunted. He questioned me about my agitation.

"Because I'm sick of telling a story probably no one believes. It sounds more ridiculous every time I say it out loud. It is stupid and embarrassing. I cannot even believe this story is the story of my miserable life," I said as I fought back tears.

"I have no idea if I can help you, but I won't know if you don't tell me what has been going on. Chances are, there will be something we can do to help you find relief, but it is up to you to take the first step in that direction."

His lack of urgency to label me as crazy made me feel comfortable enough to talk. *This guy has probably heard some bizarre stuff, so maybe my story won't be as bad as the others.*

I used the entire hour to explain the details of my corrupt brain and life. I went into detail about the bad physical feelings and how I thought they were connected with the fear of throwing up and turning gay. I told him how the suicide attempt created the bad feelings as well. I told him how I believed God would punish and reward me with the bad thoughts and feelings when I had sinned or offended him. I also told him it was God who wanted me to die. I never believed it was possible to disclose all of these details to another person. My story sounded ridiculous, but I knew it was very real and serious for me. I hoped he took my vulnerability seriously as well.

He was taking notes furiously as I concluded my story with being put in that hospital. The room went silent as I anxiously waited for his response.

"Are you going to say anything about what I've told you?" I asked.

"Well, this is a lot of information to process, and I have some thoughts and ideas about it. We will talk further at our next session."

I glared at him, puzzled and pissed off. *What in the hell? I just spilled every secret I have had in my entire life and he wants to WAIT UNTIL OUR NEXT SESSION TO HELP ME? Does he not take any of this seriously?*

"Okay, whatever Doc," I said passive-aggressively while standing up to leave.

"Chrissie, these things take time to work out. We will figure out how to help you get some relief. You have to be patient."

I flung around and stared directly in his face. "Patient? Oh okay, I'll be PATIENT. I have waited over twelve YEARS to have enough courage to kill myself and end my misery. I failed at suicide and now I am here hoping beyond anything some sort of miracle might happen and I may possibly be okay. Sorry, I'm not so patient right now. I WISH YOU KNEW WHAT IT WAS LIKE LIVING IN MY HEAD EVEN FOR A MINUTE! IT'S TORTURE! YOU HAVE NO IDEA WHAT IT'S LIKE TO LIVE THIS WAY! IT'S MISERABLE!" I shouted.

I turned around in fury, fighting back tears, and storming out as fast as my stomach would allow me to walk.

I hobbled angrily toward my room. It took absolute concentration to hold back the tears. I didn't want any of the crazy people to see me cry. I approached the TV room, wanting to see if the African-American man with glasses was still there, but was too upset to look. Stumbling into my room, I turned off the lights, and slammed the door. I barely got under the covers before the door opened behind me. It was the nurse reminding me that I was not allowed to close the door all the way.

"I KNOW," I shouted, "PLEASE JUST LEAVE ME ALONE RIGHT NOW!'

I wasn't going to move from my bed for the rest of the day. I didn't care if I needed to be part of the stupid activities. It was clear to me there was no help for who I was and I had to just get used to being institutionalized for the rest of my life. This is my life and I have to deal with it. I am defeated. How can I allow myself to believe there is hope? I am a bad person as evidenced by the signs and proof from God. I don't deserve a good life. The bad thoughts and feelings are a direct result of that. I am a failure. I am a disappointment. I have let down my entire family. I will always be alone. I need to accept the fact that it will never get better for me.

The air felt heavy. So did my heart. Sadness overwhelmed me. I was terrified and lonely.

I closed my eyes, begging for sleep. I wanted to escape the truth that I would never get better and never get out of there. I rolled over, staring out the window at the woods in the distance. *I will never enjoy the outside world again. I am stuck in my brain and this hospital forever. I should have stayed in the creek. I should never have believed there was hope. There is no hope. I am trapped. My life is over.*

Chapter 25: 'This is a Normal Brain. This is YOUR Brain'

A loud knock on my door startled me awake. The light turned on and I squinted to see who the jerk was waking me up.

"Can I come in?" my psychologist asked without waiting for me to agree.

"Um, okay."

"There is something I want to tell you, and I don't want to wait until our next session," he said.

I pulled back, frightened. *Oh God, here it is. He's going to tell me I have to come out of the closet.*

He sensed my fear and reassured me not to be afraid, that it was good news.

Pulling out a pad of paper and a pencil he proceeded to draw two brains.

He described how sometimes people who have 'normal' brains get thoughts they find intrusive or disturbing. When this happens, they have a puzzled or negative reaction, but reject the thought and dismiss it. After that initial thought, they do not react to it because they recognize it as 'unwanted and bizarre'.

He drew an arrow to represent the unwanted thought over the 'normal' person's brain and out the back.

Describing my case, he explained I may get a disturbing thought causing me to feel negative, but instead of being able to dismiss it, the thought becomes stuck like a broken record. I may question why the thought is there and want to do anything I can to make it go away. If I cannot get rid of the thought, I might experience symptoms of anxiety out of desperation. Once the thought reappears, I react with anxiety and fear at just the thought of thinking the thought. The thought will then begin to appear 'real' because I cannot figure out how to stop thinking about it regardless how irrational it may be.

He drew an arrow to represent the unwanted thought on the second brain diagram in a continuous circle around the brain, stuck like a broken record.

Should I believe this? It sounds exactly like what I experience. Is he lying? Did he just make all this up to make me feel better? Can I trust him?

His enthusiasm was infectious. I wanted to believe him so badly. What he said described the last twelve years of my life. Was it true the bad thoughts were not my fault for being a bad person? I felt a small sensation of heat in the pit of my stomach. It was a small flame of hope, and I desperately wanted to hang onto it believing there could actually be a reason why all this had happened. Was this real, or was he just making it up because he felt bad for me?

"Chrissie, what I believe you are suffering from is Obsessive-Compulsive Disorder."

My hope was shattered.

"Obsessive-Compulsive Disorder?" I asked. "I studied that in psych class. That is the disorder when people wash their hands a thousand times a day. Yeah, I wash my hands if I'm worried I may throw up, but I am not one of those people. They are nuts."

"Yes Chrissie, OCD is commonly known as the 'hand-washing disorder', but it can manifest in different ways, not just about germs and hand-washing."

I was skeptical. I wanted to believe, but it couldn't be that easy. He seemed to be an intelligent man, but how could he rattle off a diagnosis and expect everything to just be okay now? What would that even mean if I had a mental illness? On the one hand, it would mean all of this crap was not my fault, thank goodness. But, what did it mean for my future? *I am mentally ill. Is there a cure? Will I ever be able to get rid of these horrible thoughts? How could I have a normal life now that I'm a mentally ill person? If it is a mental illness, how can I ever trust my own brain? How can I know what is real and what isn't real? Does this mean everything I believe is a lie?*

He recognized how deeply distressed I was as I thought. He asked me to keep the diagram and said we would talk further at our next session. In the meantime, I should read books and articles about OCD in the patient library. He said there were many treatment options for OCD, and he truly believed we would be able to find relief for my symptoms.

He left the room all smiles. I stared at the diagrams. It made sense. Everything he said about the 'bad brain' was exactly what it felt like for me. But, how could a diagnosis be the cause of all this misery? How could the answer be this simple? Wouldn't I just know if I had a brain disorder? All of my thoughts and fears seemed real. My body even reacted to them. What if that meant I really didn't have OCD but he just thought I did? Did that mean there was absolutely no hope for me?

I sunk under the covers tucking the diagram tightly against my chest. The moonlight streamed in my window where I could see bushes outlined against the glass. I hadn't noticed them until then and I had been there almost a week. A slow smile crept across my face.

Is it possible I could be okay? Is it possible I could actually have a normal life without all of this misery and chaos in my mind?

I wanted to believe. I clutched the diagram across my chest and prayed in what seemed like a very long time:

Oh please God, let this be the answer. Please let it be something not completely my fault and I can get help for. Please, I will do anything if this could be the answer.

For the first time in months, I went to sleep with an authentic sense of hope.

Chapter 26: I *Am* One of These People

I woke to sunlight streaming into my room. I rolled over and saw the crumpled diagram of my brain. I stared at it again. *Could this be true?* I felt a twinge of excitement, but didn't want to feel overly hopeful. There was a chance this guy could be wrong, and I didn't want to put faith in this idea until I had proof.

I looked into the hallway and saw all the crazy people heading to the cafeteria. I put on my brown, corduroy overalls, stumbled toward the door, and followed the herd down the hallway. Today felt different - oddly optimistic. I wondered if it was fleeting, like the intermittent breaks I had over the last few weeks before the suicide attempt. I didn't want to put too much stock in this new feeling of hope and optimism, but decided to enjoy it in the moment.

Before today, I had either demanded food in my room or not eaten at all, so the cafeteria was a new experience. I grabbed a tray and walked into the big room with the tables. It felt like high school again but instead of popular crowds, it was lunatic cliques. I saw the African-American guy with the glasses and wondered what he would do if I sat at his table. I cautiously walked over to his table and sat at the very end.

"Hey there!' he said. "Why don't you scoot down here and join us?"

I looked at everyone else for their approval, and they waved me over.

How could these people want anything to do with me after the complete brat I had been over the past week? I had snubbed them in the halls, avoided group meetings, and even given them dirty looks in the medication line.

"What's your name?"

"Chrissie."

"We've all been wondering if you were ever going to try to talk to us," he said jokingly and everyone giggled.

I felt embarrassed and ashamed, but he did not skip a beat. He introduced himself as Rob and rattled off the names of everyone else at the table. They were gracious and welcoming. I was grateful after how badly I had treated them.

Rob told me he has bipolar with psychotic features. I stared blankly at him as he told me his diagnosis so confidently. Who the hell would admit that so freely? *He must really be nuts.* He told his story about almost jumping in front of the MARTA train at a downtown station. He realized he was relapsing after how close he came to jumping, and that is how he ended up here.

One by one, individuals disclosed their diagnosis and reasons for being in the hospital. They talked about their families, their lives back home, and their jobs. I listened in disbelief. They were cracking jokes and laughing. They'd talk seriously, and then tease each other sensitively but supportively.

These are normal people. These are everyday individuals you would see at the grocery store or the mall. They aren't the 'One Flew Over the Cuckoo's Nest' kind of people.

The conversation halted as everyone stared at me.

"Well, Chrissie, why are you here?" asked Jason, a self-disclosed borderline personality disorder sufferer.

"Um...well...I, um...think I have some kind of disorder..."

"Oooh!" Rob said sarcastically, "This must be your first time in a psychiatric facility!"

Everyone started to chuckle. I felt embarrassed and wanted to leave, feeling hot and not being able to breathe.

Jason recognized my discomfort and put his hand on my arm.

"Chrissie, it is very scary the first time you are in the hospital. We all had preconceived notions about what kind of people would be here and whether or not they would be psycho killers."

Everyone nodded and laughed. I started to relax a bit.

"Did you try to kill yourself?" Rob asked.

I was appalled at his pointed question.

"The reason I asked is because you don't seem to be walking comfortably. What did you do?"

If anyone else had asked me, I believe I would have run away crying. But there was something about Rob that made me feel comfortable. There was an overwhelming sense of compassion and empathy. I knew I could be forthcoming with him and still be accepted.

I gave them an overview without details about the creek. I told them the doctor thought I may have Obsessive-Compulsive Disorder, but wasn't sure I believed him. They assured me my psychologist was trustworthy and I should start treatment as soon as possible. Their approval and input helped me feel better.

After breakfast, I walked with the group to the medication line. Rob didn't leave my side. He talked and laughed the whole time. I liked him so much. He felt like a friend already.

I started going to group sessions scheduled throughout the day. The only reason I went was because attendance was required if I wanted to get out of there. The groups were terribly condescending.

Most of them were run by young interns. They talked to us like we were little kids with a punishment/reward system. I barely participated because I didn't want to give them the satisfaction of believing they knew anything about what we had been through. It was infuriating to listen to them talk to us like we were idiots. I usually sat in the back of the room, staring with disdain at the instructor. After a while, they knew not to call on me or ask for my input. I experienced a mix of emotions. On the one hand, I felt smarter than them in regards to understanding the effects of mental illness. On the other, the groups caused me to feel small, insignificant, and worthless.

During downtime, I sat timidly in the milieu trying to be friendly. The people I had shunned never flinched and took the opportunity to introduce themselves to me. They started with their names, diagnoses, and why they were there. I met people with bipolar, borderline personality disorder, depression, and Post Traumatic Stress Disorder. They were normal, everyday people, who talked about their lives back home and what they would be doing for Christmas if they weren't in the hospital. It seemed the common conduit on the unit was suicidal thoughts or attempted suicide.

At times after therapy sessions or groups, I saw patients open up to each other with tears, anger, and frustration about their illnesses. Other patients would step in, providing comfort and reassurance. They would cry with the individual. They would empathize. They would hold their hand.

I stayed quiet. I felt like a jerk. I had judged these people. Now they were willing to include and embrace me even though I shunned and treated them like dirt. They were better than I was, even though I thought the opposite when I arrived. I could not deny I was one of these people deemed mentally ill, but I wished I could be as good as they were to each other. I wanted to try. I wanted to be better.

Every day, I made an effort to reach out and talk to someone. I didn't talk about my own story, but wanted to know what they had been through so I listened and learned. As new people arrived, I made an effort to welcome them just as that big, wild haired girl did when I arrived. I had been so rude to her. She left before I decided to be nice, and I wished I had the opportunity to apologize to her.

The positive effects of medication began to kick in after a couple of weeks. As the fog and sadness lifted, I felt optimistic. It made me realize perhaps I had been suffering from depression. Sessions with the psychologist focused on managing the bad thoughts. His advice did not really help, but I wasn't worried because the medication was helping everything seem better.

The side effects of Prozac were horrendous. I was nauseous all day, which increased my anxiety about possibly throwing up. I had no appetite. I had insomnia. Luckily, I made friends with the night manager and he allowed me to hang outside my room at night until I felt tired. It was torture staying in my room with nothing to do while I couldn't sleep. So, I walked up and down the halls. There was another guy who couldn't sleep sometimes either, so we'd meet up, watch late night TV together, and eat prepackaged cups of vanilla ice cream with small wooden spoons. We'd laugh at the stupid shows and crack jokes making each other laugh. Oddly enough, I actually had fun on those nights.

One afternoon in the milieu, Rob hollered at me to leave for lunch. I stood up quickly, and walked toward the hallway. I took five steps when everything turned fuzzy and black. I couldn't feel my body. I saw a big flash of light and felt a big blow to my head like someone had whacked me in the back of the head with a baseball bat. When I came to, I could hear myself screaming,

"IT'S FINALLY HAPPENED! MY HEAD HAS EXPLODED! OH MY GOD, MY HEAD HAS FINALLY EXPLODED!!"

My sight slowly began to return and Rob was standing over me laughing hysterically.

"WHAT IS SO FUNNY?" I demanded as the tears began to well.

Two nurses pulled me into the sitting position stifling their laughter. They informed me about a side effect of Prozac being lightheadedness and dizziness with quick motions. I had stood up too fast, passed out, and hit my head on the wall as I fell. My head hadn't exploded, but it sure was funny for everyone to hear me screaming that it had. Rob helped me to the examining room to get checked out, and I was laughing too by the time we got there. I felt so lucky to have a friend like him there.

As time progressed, I started to feel a strong connection to the people in the hospital. I began sinking into my new skin. These were the first people to see the real me with this brain disorder, and they still liked me. They still wanted to be around me. I was terrified, but they gave me nothing to fear. They gave me hope. They liked me despite the illness. They accepted me without hesitation. I was one of the crazy mentally ill people there, and I was starting to feel less shame and embarrassment about it. A small flicker of confidence began to grow, and I had those wonderful hospital peers to thank.

I felt proud to be one of them.

Chapter 27: Your Name is WHAT?

Based on my progress and cooperation at the hospital, I was taken off suicide watch. The nurse informed me I would be moving into a shared room. I did not want this, but I knew I couldn't argue if I wanted out of there. I worried about being in a room with a complete stranger in a psychiatric facility. Would I be safe? What if they were annoying or not to be trusted?

I packed my bag and headed toward the opposite end of the unit, feeling anxious the closer I got to my new room. I had grown accustomed to my own space and hoped rooming with someone wouldn't disrupt my progress. I counted the room numbers leading up to mine. The door was closed. *Hmm, I guess once you aren't a suicide threat, you are allowed to actually close your door. That is interesting and annoying.*

I saw my name and my roommates on a card next to the door and broke into a sweat. My anxiety amped up uncontrollably. I could barely catch my breath. My name was listed on the bottom and her name was above mine:

Gaye

Chrissie

What the hell? Is this some kind of a joke? I haven't told anyone here about the obsession. Did my therapist do this as some kind of sick joke? Why would someone do this to me?

I bent over trying to breathe. *Gaye Chrissie! Is this a sign? Is this proof I have to be gay?* Half expecting to walk in and see my therapist smiling or laughing, I slowly opened the door hoping this was a practical joke.

My twin bed was neatly made in front of me, and there was a second twin bed in the corner. I saw a woman sitting with her back facing me. She was reading and didn't look up when the door opened. I could tell she was petite, older, and her hair looked like curly 'mom' hair. I was trying to contain my anxiety about her name actually being 'Gaye', worrying it was some sort of sign. I didn't want her to see me upset. I dropped my bag on the bed, and bolted to the bathroom. I washed my face, trying to compose myself. *How am I going to talk to her? How did this happen? Is this really happening? Is my roommate's name really 'Gaye'?*

I took a deep breath and walked back into the room trying not to look at her. She didn't move. It was weird that she had her back turned to me. Then I remembered how I felt the first day I arrived. I had hated everyone and I hated myself. Maybe she was just shy and scared?

It was against everything I wanted to say her name out loud, but I figured I needed to try to be nice since she was new.

"Hi there, is your name……um……uh………Gaye?" I asked, my palms sweated profusely and my breathing close to hyperventilating. I couldn't believe I had said it out loud.

"Yes," she answered shyly.

God, I have seriously gotten paired with someone actually named Gaye! What the hell?

"I'm Chrissie."

She didn't reply.

There was no better time to escape, so I got up to find Rob and my other friends. I could barely handle the anxiety about her name anyway, so all I wanted to do was get out of that room.

"I.....I just don't want to be here right now," she said shakily. "All I want is to be with my family on Christmas, but I cannot manage this depression. I cannot do it. I just feel so sad."

I stopped at the door, turning toward her. She was still facing the wall and I noticed how badly her hands were shaking.

I returned and sat on my bed.

"Tell me about your family," I asked.

She closed her book, turning halfway in my direction as she wiped tears from underneath her glasses onto her jacket. She told me about her two daughters and her face lit up as she mentioned them. She shared how they were so important to her, and she felt a disappointment to them as a mother because she was in a psychiatric hospital over Christmas.

I wanted to hug her and tell her it would be okay, but anxiety about her name kept me from moving. Part of me wanted to chuckle at the unbelievable coincidence. I knew the repercussions my mind might present if I got near someone named 'Gaye', so I just listened from across the room.

When she finished talking about her family, I told her about the cool people I had met there and how I could introduce her. In my mind, I knew I would actually introduce them to her and she could introduce herself, so I wouldn't have to say her name out loud.

After talking for a while, my anxiety had dramatically lessened by the time I left the room. I thought it was interesting how sitting in the horrible, uncomfortable anxiety actually made it go away. I would have expected the opposite. Whenever I recalled the door with her name on it or even the room itself though, I experienced an intense spike in anxiety. I hoped it would lessen each time like it did today or it was going to be hard for me the remainder of my stay there.

As I stood up to leave, she called my name. I turned around as she faced me and thanked me for taking the time to listen. She was grateful for a roommate who understood. Walking down the hall, I reflected how I truly couldn't believe my roommate's name was 'Gaye'. I also couldn't believe how parallel our feelings were about disappointing everyone for being in the hospital. It was a relief to know someone else felt that way too. We had a common experience of shame and guilt, but felt lucky to be surrounded by people who understood. I shook my head and chuckled at how scared I was entering the room previously, and how comforted I felt upon leaving. Her name didn't mean anything to me anymore. We were in the same situation, fighting a similar, lonely battle. I felt lucky to have a roommate who understood the complexity of the stigma surrounding mental illness, despite her uncomfortable name.

Chapter 28: I Am Worthy of Love

I introduced my friends to Gaye that evening, being careful not to say her name. She fit right in and before she knew it, was replacing her tears with comfort and laughter, just as I had.

Every evening after group sessions finished, we had the option of gathering in the milieu to socialize, play games, and/or watch an educational film about mental health. Tonight, I was barely paying attention to the film on the television, until I heard a lady saying she experienced questions all day starting with 'What if?'

"Quiet everyone!" I asserted.

I scooted toward the television. Three people were telling their stories of mental health. Each story seemed bizarrely similar to the last twelve years of my life. The fears weren't the same but their reactions, worries, and anxieties matched perfectly.

Then I heard it.

"Each one of the individual's stories you have heard suffer with Obsessive-Compulsive Disorder."

I gasped loudly, covering my face with my hands. Rob walked over and sat beside me. He put his arm around me. I looked at him with eyes wide open.

"Is this you, Chrissie?" he asked.

"I think. I hope. I believe it is, Rob," I said.

I began to cry. Within seconds, there were at least five people comforting me.

"I'm okay. I'm just happy and just relieved. I'm just happy something is wrong with my brain and none of this is my fault!"

Everyone seemed relieved I was crying out of happiness instead of having a breakdown. Someone handed me a tissue and I turned to face the group.

"Tell us about your OCD," Rob asked.

I felt panicked. *What if I tell them and they hate me afterward? What if I tell them and they don't believe it is OCD? What if they believe the thoughts are real?*

But, these people had given me no reason not to trust them. They had been so vulnerable with me about their stories. So, I took a deep breath and began telling my story. I looked up to see the clinicians in the milieu walking over wanting to hear it as well. Apparently I had been somewhat of a mystery to everyone there.

"It started when I was eight years old sitting in my 3rd grade classroom..."

I told the entire story up to the moment I stepped foot in the mental hospital.

"And, now I am here with y'all," I said with my head down. I stared at the floor waiting for a reaction. I waited for anything. I began to feel panic as the silence drug on. I hoped my worst fears of being rejected and hated hadn't come true.

After what seemed like an hour of silence, Rob started chuckling. I looked at him with fear and confusion. *Why is he laughing about what I have been through?* Tears of regret began to well up in my eyes.

"So after everything you've been through, you get to the psych ward and they put you with a roommate named Gaye?" he said.

The entire group erupted in laughter.

"Now that's just cruel!" he joked with uncontrollable laughter.

Gaye was trying to apologize for her name, but couldn't get the words out, she was laughing so hard.

The heaviest weight lifted off my back.

No one cared about my obsessions. No one judged me about anything I had been through. Each person came over and hugged me. Several of them told me how grateful they were I had survived the suicide attempt. Others told me they knew people who lived with and managed OCD. And several others just thanked me for being honest and sharing my story.

These were the first friends who knew all my deepest and darkest secrets, and didn't see me differently. I had kept these fears a secret for so long afraid of rejection and judgment. Now I could see it had no bearing on whether or not I deserved or was capable of receiving love. I sat amongst these friends with awe and gratitude.

Afterward, we watched a movie together, and before they retired to their rooms they hugged me, thanking me for my vulnerability. No one cared about that horrible part of me. They cared about me. My disorder did not change my value to them.

The next morning I woke up to blue sky peeking through my window. Life had color again. I had friends who loved everything about me, even the things I believed were unlovable. Life seemed different, in a better way.

I walked into the milieu hoping the feeling from the night before carried over, and I got my wish. I felt even more connected to the patients and staff. The level of intimacy and acceptance was rewarding, soothing and something I never believed I would be worthy of receiving. All my vulnerable walls had come tumbling down, and I was still accepted and loved.

At lunch, I walked onto the stage and uncovered the piano I had stared at every day. Sitting down, I played a memorized Bach two-part invention for the patients and staff. I received a standing ovation. I had something to offer. I mattered. I was worthy of living. I stood up, playfully bowed, and looked at Rob and my other friends knowing they were proud of me. Tears of joy welled up.

Later that evening, my friends and I were sitting on the floor next to the horribly decorated, ugly Christmas tree, talking about what we would be doing for Christmas if we weren't stuck there. While talking, I started looking at the ornaments on the tree and noticed that every ornament was broken or cracked in some place. I started laughing uncontrollably.

"WHAT? WHAT!!?" they asked.

Once I caught my breath I said, "As if we need one more reason to know we are completely screwed up and broken, we get shitty, broken ornaments!?"

Everyone laughed so hard.

It was ironic. All I wanted three weeks ago was to be dead because I was lonely, miserable, and full of fear. Now, here I was, the week of Christmas in a mental institution with certifiably 'crazy' people, feeling more loved, accepted, and full of hope than I had ever experienced before in my life.

There was no place I would rather have been during those holidays. The very people I had turned my nose up to when I first arrived had saved my life. They taught me not only to love myself, but how powerful loving others can be. They taught me by being selfless and letting go of pride you can discover true humanity. They taught me never to judge anyone by how they looked on the outside or what their name was. They taught me taking risks and having faith in people can pay off. But most importantly, they taught me no matter how 'normal' someone looks or acts, you never know how badly they may be suffering.

The individuals I met in the psychiatric hospital were my introduction to the importance of peers, and how valuable shared experiences can enrich our lives. I knew the experiences I had with my hospital peers would lay the groundwork for who I was to become as I reentered the real world with the new label of mental illness. If I could find this love and support in the hospital, I knew it was possible to find it on the outside.

Chapter 29: Institutionalized

The medication was taking full effect. I felt more optimistic, hopeful, and confident every day. My psychologist was ready to discharge me. I was excited and nervous. I desperately wanted to feel the freedom of being outside those locked doors, but would be walking into a completely different life. The hospital was safe and I felt accepted there. Outside, I wasn't sure I would receive the same response.

Also, I was sad to leave my friends. We promised to stay in touch, but I had doubts we would want to be reminded of the Christmas we spent in the psych ward. The night before my departure was bittersweet. I wanted to savor the laughter and tears. I cried with mixed emotions as I packed. Gaye sat on her bed crying with me. I was an entirely different person now than when I arrived there. During my stay, the curtain was lifted from my eyes allowing me to see the world through different lenses. Would my old life accept this new Chrissie?

The next morning, as I sat in silence in the milieu with my friends, I saw my dad and sister walk through the door. They seemed like strangers. I hugged each of my friends one by one. The last was Rob. He had changed my life. I pulled back from him and expressed my deepest thanks. He didn't respond, but I knew he understood. Holding back tears, he squeezed my hands and nodded toward the door. I picked up my bags and looked back at them as I walked out the door. They waved at me while I wiped the tears from my face. *How am I so sad to leave? When I arrived, I wanted nothing more than to be anywhere but here? Now, I wish I could stay.* I was confused.

I climbed into the backseat of the car. I felt like an alien, not knowing where I belonged. No one in the car knew what to say to make the moment less awkward. I didn't want to speak about my experience, so I pressed my forehead against the cold window and watched the trees whip by. Joy talked the whole time, thank goodness. She took the pressure off me to talk about how I knew I had screwed up everyone's Christmas.

We arrived at the medical hospital for an appointment to remove the staples in my stomach. Walking through the doors of the hospital brought back memories of the suicide attempt. I felt anxiety creeping up, but I remembered to breathe and think about my time at the psych hospital, my diagnosis, and my friends.

We were taken to an exam room, enduring a long bout of awkward silence before my emergency room doctor came in. I felt relieved to see him as he flashed a smile at me. He seemed relieved to see how well I was doing considering the last time he saw me. He chatted with us as he popped the staples out of my stomach. It was surreal to watch him do this. The six inch surgical incision and stab opening had healed well. He seemed pleased with my recovery. I wanted to tell him everything was okay and I had OCD and I wasn't really just crazy. But, he was busy and couldn't linger to chat.

I felt disappointed. I wanted to explain what really happened. I wanted him to know my actions weren't my fault. I wanted him to know I valued life and hadn't intentionally wanted this to happen. I wanted his reassurance and approval. I didn't get it, and it felt like something was missing without him knowing the truth. I left the hospital feeling down.

The closer we got to daddy's house, the more anxiety I experienced. I hadn't seen the house since the night I was in the muddy bathtub. How would it feel to be back? I closed my eyes and thought about my friends at the hospital. It was after lunch, so they were probably hanging outside smoking or in the TV room talking and laughing. I wished I was there with them where it was safe and I was loved.

We pulled into the driveway, and flashbacks of that night came flooding into my mind. I pictured myself standing in the middle of the road shoving the knife in my sock. I remembered how the air sparkled like suspended glitter in the cold. I could almost feel how cold the air had felt as I breathed it in on the first step out the door. I wished I could go back to that night and talk myself out of it. I wished I could tell myself to ask for help instead of attempting suicide. I could have prevented ruining my relationship with my family. I could have saved them from all the anger and pain they must feel toward me.

The tension was palpable when I entered the house. Linda was waiting for us and I could barely look at her. I imagined how frustrated she must be with me. I hadn't seen her since my surgery. She had never wanted kids in the first place, and I don't believe what happened made her feel warm and fuzzy about me. I was grateful she acted glad I was home. It was less awkward for me.

I went straight to my room. Walking down the hallway made the flashbacks increase. I remembered stashing the knife behind the toaster. I thought about creeping downstairs quietly. The bathroom brought me back to being in the tub. I hurried past the bathroom refusing to look inside. Walking into my room, I looked over at the bright, red numbers on my clock that had summoned me to get up and kill myself.

I remembered the pact I made with God on that night. I hadn't thought about God much since all this happened. I had no idea where my relationship with Him stood and I had zero desire to figure it out. If I really had OCD, all of my beliefs were now convoluted and questionable. The thought of untangling everything I thought I knew and believed seemed way too daunting to figure out anytime soon. It also made me feel angry, and I didn't want to address that anger at that moment.

I squeezed my eyes shut attempting to shake the thoughts and memories. I pulled off my shoes and climbed into bed. I missed the hospital. There, I was able to be myself. I was part of a group. I was an important person to others. I was a good friend. People enjoyed being around me.

Here at home, I felt awkward, like I didn't belong, like my presence made it weird for everyone. It seemed as if they were masking their anger at me and what had happened. *Didn't they know I did not ask for this disorder? Didn't they know that I could not help thinking and acting the way I did? Do they think I wanted to be like this? Do they care at all how hard this is on me?*

I felt embarrassed and ashamed for the suicide attempt and the disorder I suffered with. I felt guilty for letting it get so out of hand and not asking for help. *But, I didn't know there was help for me. I didn't know there were other people out there like me. How could I have known it without saying it out loud? My brain warned me for years about saying it out loud. I was scared!*

I wished I was back in the hospital where everything felt easier. *I am not important here at home. I am not wanted here. I am a burden here. I feel like everyone thinks crazy daughter Chrissie is back from the mental home.* I missed my friends and wanted to go back.

I drifted to sleep.

I awoke to knocking at my door. Linda popped her head in reminding me of the church service we would be attending that night.

Oh, crap. The last thing I want to do is put on a fake smile after getting out of the psych ward! I was tired of being a fake. I had done that for too long. I was done pretending to be someone I wasn't. I wasn't ready to go in public and try to make it appear like everything was fine.

Everything isn't fine! Everything will not be fine for a while, and it is okay with me. But everyone else is going to expect me to pretend I'm all better. I am sick of pretending that life is wonderful. It's not easy, it has never been easy, and I'm tired of making it appear like it is.

I knew I had to do a daughter's duty to my minister father's reputation. I'm sure in this small town, word probably spread about the pastor's daughter going crazy one night and ending up in the looney bin. So for his sake, I'd go and pretend. I'd go and act as if we had the perfect family and the perfect life even though we were lying. *I imagine most of the congregation is lying about their lives as well. It seems like such bullshit.*

I rolled out of bed and stood up. It dawned on me I could finally stand up straight since my staples were taken out. I smiled. I was a few inches taller than I was a few days ago. I put on a red sweater and black pants, and dragged myself into the living room. Daddy had to be at the church early, so I rode with Joy and Linda.

I felt nothing but anger as I entered the church. But I smiled, nodded, and shook people's hands trying to look pretty and happy like I always pretended to be. What I really wanted to do was grab the microphone and scream to everyone that my life had been a lie. I wanted them to know how sick I had been in my head for twelve years, and that I tried to kill myself in a creek down the street, and the only people I could relate to were people in the mental home. I wanted to scream it as loud as I could and see how many people would stay, listen, and not judge me. Probably not many! I wanted to tell them who I really was instead of the façade I had been putting on for them.

Instead of grabbing the microphone, I followed my sister as we found our seats toward the front of the church. The choir filed in and I caught my grandmother's eye. She winked and smiled at me. I wondered if she hated me too. We sang a hymn and I could barely muster a note without feeling I would burst into tears. I didn't want to lose it in front of these people. I needed to uphold this stupid 'image'. I'm sure I had embarrassed my family enough with the suicide attempt, so I didn't need to make things worse then.

I looked at daddy standing in the pulpit getting ready to deliver his sermon, wondering how ashamed he must feel to be my father. I glanced at grandmother singing alto at the top of her lungs. I bet she couldn't believe what a disappointment I turned out to be. I felt Joy sitting beside me, her arm through mine. She was probably so ashamed of me, but doesn't want me to embarrass them any more than I already had. She was probably just pretending to care about me.

I couldn't hold it in any longer.

How was I going to process the overwhelming emotions attached to the last several weeks. I wanted to be angry. I wanted to be sad. I wanted to be confused. I wanted to feel relief. I wanted to feel hope. I had no idea where to start. So, I just started crying. I bent over in the pew and cried so hard I could barely breathe. Joy put her arm around me. I was grateful the hymn had so many verses so I could get it all out before daddy started preaching.

Where would my life go from here? I had one foot tied to the comfort and safety of the psych hospital, and the other was anxious to jump back into the real world and forget all that had happened. I didn't know how I would find the strength or energy to launch off the starting blocks.

I wanted to trust the process. I wanted to believe something good would come out of this. But re-entering the world I used to know at twenty years old knowing everything I believed about reality wasn't true seemed daunting and terrifying. I felt stuck in the middle of a life I once knew and the new life I needed to create. I had no understanding of who I had been and who I now was. Everything I had believed, acted, and reacted to was based on lies. Perception of my beliefs and the world was a farce. How could I trust anything I thought? How was I to carry on from here? I hoped somehow I would be able to find the same acceptance, love, and understanding I had felt in the hospital. I hoped I would be strong enough to be okay after all that had happened.

I hoped I could find resolution. I hoped there was a purpose. I hoped something, anything good, could come from this. I hoped all this didn't happen in vain. *Please let there be a happy ending.*

Chapter 30: Let's Pretend Nothing Happened!

It was strange trying to integrate back into 'reality' after leaving the hospital. I was astounded at how easy it was for my family and me to ignore everything that had taken place. Christmas and New Year's came and went and we pretended I was all better now. Part of me wanted it this way, but the other part of me was screaming for acknowledgement and empathy for the suffering I had endured. I was conflicted about wanting compassion while not wanting to be victimized.

I returned to Georgia Southern University winter quarter as a different individual. I had lost fifteen pounds, had a six inch scar on my stomach, and a fresh perspective on life. I also had an arsenal of lies to distribute when questioned about this new person.

I did not want everyone to know about my Christmas break experience. I disclosed the details to three people in case I relapsed and needed support. I told my roommate Allison, my friend Brad, and my cross-country partner Meredith. I was terrified to tell them, worrying they would judge me or decide I was not worth having as a friend. Surprisingly, all three of them accepted the news with empathy, compassion, and love. I was grateful and relieved.

I made up a story about stomach problems and emergency exploratory surgery to anyone else who asked what happened. Surprisingly, no one questioned its validity.

As I settled back into college life, I began questioning everything my beliefs, rituals, and ruminations had taught me. If I really had OCD, 'living a good Christian life' to avoid being punished by the bad thoughts had no validity. Although the thought of deviating from the behavior I had practiced and perfected for twelve years seemed terrifying, I wanted to test and see if it was really OCD. I wanted to see if my skewed way of thinking about God and being punished had been actual nonsense or if there was some proof. With the medication working so well, I should be able to tell by dabbling in what I would have deemed as 'sinful' behavior worthy of punishment before.

The first test would be alcohol. Pre-OCD, I had believed this to be a horrible sin warranting punishment by God. However, if I drank alcohol and didn't have the bad thoughts, it might 'prove' I actually did have OCD. It would also 'prove' everything I had believed about God was a fallacy. I wasn't sure how to process the depth and magnitude of that discovery if it were true. Would I be opening Pandora's Box? Could I handle that large dose of truth right then? While I felt concerned, I concluded I would save soul-searching that problem for a later time.

I told Allison I wanted to try alcohol as we were getting ready to go out. She looked at me in disbelief. Since she had known me, I never hinted at even wanting a sip of alcohol, and now I was going for it all the way. She started laughing in excitement. I believe she was more enthusiastic about my decision than I was!

We headed to El Sombrero, one of our favorite spots. I squeezed into a crowded booth with my sorority sisters as the waiter took drink orders. No one paid attention to anyone ordering until it came to me.

"I will have a glass of White Zinfandel," I said confidently.

The table became silent. Every jaw dropped. A flurry of questions began. I laughed them off, explaining I was simply experimenting with alcohol this quarter. I didn't have the energy to explain I was actually testing the validity of a higher power and my possible mental illness. My friends were stunned, but excited. I also believed they were slightly disappointed they were losing their trusted sober driver.

The first gulp was pungent. I wasn't sure if I could finish the glass based on the taste, until it hit my stomach. I started feeling warm from the inside out. A relaxed, numb feeling coursed through my arms and legs. The table was silent as they waited for my reaction. I leaned back against the cushioned seat. "Well, this feels interesting!" Everyone laughed and started imbibing their drinks.

Wow! How have I not partaken in this before now? I can actually relax. My head feels quiet and calm. What a perfect escape!

Before I knew it, I had swigged the last sip. My head was becoming warm and fuzzy and I liked it. I was talking and laughing loudly. I was relaxed. I knew everyone was wondering what happened to create this change in me. I was adamantly against drinking because of my faith prior to this Christmas. I hoped no one would actually question me tonight or anytime soon. I wasn't sure when or if I'd ever be ready to disclose anything.

I was talking to the girls in the booth behind me when I felt a tap on my shoulder. I turned around and Allison nodded toward the table. I saw a second glass of White Zinfandel in front of me as the girls at the table started giggling. I guess they wanted to see what drunk Chrissie would look like. I wondered if I wanted to find out.

Do I want to do this? Is it safe? Am I really ready to test this theory? YES, I AM. The brain disorder OCD causes the horrible thoughts, the horrible rituals and ruminations, and my inability to lead a life independently of it. It has NOTHING to do with God. It has NOTHING to do with me being a bad person. It's time to start living life away from fearing God.

I debated back and forth, worrying about repercussions. I had been programmed by OCD for so long, I did not know any other way than to worry when I felt like I was doing something *wrong* according to my 'beliefs'. I was so brainwashed thinking bad thoughts were about being a bad person, that I was feeling actual panic at the thought of being defiantly assertive for my own interest.

Eight-year-old Chrissie was screaming inside of me, warning my actions would cause a horrific reaction. Fear and guilt began rising inside of me. My chest shivered and the air felt like it was being sucked out of my lungs. What if I threw up? I excused myself to the ladies room.

I swung the 'Women's' door open, bending down to check the stalls for feet. I normally did this, checking for feet turned toward the toilet indicating someone may be throwing up, to see if I needed to escape. This time, I was making sure I was alone. The stalls were empty. I swung around and stared at myself in the mirror.

You are NOT miserable, ridiculous Chrissie anymore. You are NOT the stupid girl who is afraid of life pigeonholed by ridiculous fears that aren't real. You survived a suicide attempt. You spent weeks in a psychiatric ward. YOU have a brain disorder and YOU are not going to let the lies rule your life anymore. Remember what you went through and stop being afraid. This is your life now. Take control of it. Do what you want and forget everything else.

My breathing calmed. My face was flushed, but electrified from the alcohol. I washed my hands, fluffed my hair, and took one more look at my face. A sly smile crept across it. *Let's see if this OCD thing is real.*

I went out to the table, sat down with my friends, and toasted the second glass of wine to a new and fun winter semester.

It was time to start living.

Chapter 31: I Don't Need Meds Anymore!

A mixture of exploration and untangling a lifetime of false beliefs became my journey. Every 'sin' and 'bad thing' I believed would cause punishment no longer mattered. This was overwhelming. There were no correlations between my behaviors and thoughts as I had previously believed. The truth was exciting, but frightening. OCD was so deeply entrenched in my life it was hard to separate the lies from who I was as an individual. In fact, I didn't know who I was at all. I had never made decisions based on what I wanted; I had only made decisions to avoid bad thoughts and feelings.

A mixture of excitement and anger accompanied this notion. On the one hand, a new world opened up without the burden and stress of constant anxiety. But on the other, frustration and anger simmered for the years I had lost to OCD. I needed to address and grieve the loss of the twelve years engrossed in OCD, but I wasn't ready to open those floodgates. I chose to enjoy life without symptoms while flying high on meds. And, I had a blast doing it.

I spent summer at Camp Glisson again. It was like night and day compared to the previous summer with depression. I felt care-free and high on life. Many times when kids became sick I experienced anxiety, but the medication helped so much by lessening my need to engage in compulsions. I truly believed life was different now and I'd never deal with OCD again.

I quickly fell head over heels for Keith. He was tall, handsome, hilarious, and our chemistry was off the charts. We spent the summer in a whirlwind of a romance that only seemed like the blink of an eye before it was over. Keith attended a university nine hours away from my college. Since we were both student athletes with autumn sports seasons, we knew the chance of having a lasting relationship was slim to none.

We decided to keep in touch and hope for the best, but I quickly learned my heart belonged to him. I was devastated leaving him to return for fall semester. The thought of being unable to see him for months was heart breaking. I refused to even think about dating anyone else. Not being with him was unfathomable. We talked every few days, trying not to lose touch. It was a tough semester.

A few weeks into the semester, I was convinced medication wasn't necessary. I reasoned just knowing my thoughts were due to OCD should make them manageable. How could I actually believe the thoughts were real when I knew they were caused by OCD? Also, I hated the side effects, especially the sexual ones. They made me feel like nothing sexual was arousing or enjoyable. I knew I would see Keith at Thanksgiving, and wanted to enjoy being intimate. So, I weaned myself off Prozac. *What could it really hurt? It's not like I'd ever be as sick as I was last year, right?*

Thanksgiving and Christmas breaks were magical. I loved being with Keith again. My feelings for him were real and intense. I was happy we decided to stay in touch. I felt a nagging depressive feeling creeping in though, and it bothered me. I assumed I was just sad remembering the events of last Christmas, so I ignored it. I was sure it was just temporary and would soon pass.

Facing a long distance relationship, I wasn't looking forward to winter semester. I cried the entire drive to Georgia Southern. It would be over a month before I would see Keith again, which seemed agonizing. The dark, depressive feeling was growing stronger. I attributed it to grief over leaving Keith, but something inside didn't trust those instincts.

The excitement of the new semester was in full swing, but I couldn't shake feelings of sadness and fear. When I talked to Keith, the anticipation and happiness I usually felt began waning. Friends wanted me to go out, but I didn't have the energy or desire. I always loved winter cross-country season, but this year I dreaded practice and socializing with my teammates. Assuming I was tired and sad about Keith, I ignored the blaring warning signs.

The first day of classes arrived, and I entered the Psychology building looking for my Statistics class. I poked my head in the classroom, scanning to see if I knew anyone. *Dang it, there's no one I know in here.* A guy in the back caught my eye. I had never seen him before, and couldn't take my eyes off him. He had jet black hair, piercing dark eyes, wild hair, and a bull nose ring. I blushed as he looked directly at me. He wore a leather jacket and a motorcycle helmet sat on the desk beside him. *Damn, I wish I could sit next to him.* I didn't want to make my attraction obvious by asking him to move his helmet when other seats were available. He was gorgeous. I stole glances at him as I moved through the class to an open seat. I knew he was aware of my admiration the way his eyes followed me.

Something broke my fixation on him. A girl walked into the room glancing at the desks. Locking eyes with me, she smiled and waved. I returned her smile awkwardly because I had never seen her before. Since she was wearing a Kappa Delta jersey, I thought maybe I knew her from sorority rush. She came barreling toward me, plopping down in the seat in front of me. Turning around, she leaned so close to my face I could smell her lip gloss. A surge of panic shot through me and I quickly pulled back. My anxiety jolted me back in my seat. She was saying something about how she didn't want to sit by anyone who wasn't cool, but I could barely comprehend her sentences.

Why do I feel panicked? I began questioning why I worried about her being close to me. *Did I like her being this close? What if I did? Did I want her to be? Why would I worry about whether or not she was in my space? If I wanted her close to me, why would I feel panicked that* she was? *Was her being so close making me attracted to her? Did I think she was pretty? Oh my God...what are these thoughts?*

"Um, do I know you?" I asked.

"Nope, but I saw that you had an Alpha Delta Pi hat on, so I figured you were cool and wanted to sit by you."

I cursed my stupid hat. *Why didn't I just take a shower this morning instead of wearing this hat?* She kept talking to me with her face awkwardly close to mine. I didn't want to move so she wouldn't suspect I was uncomfortable, which might have meant I had reason to feel uncomfortable, but I didn't want her to know that or have any idea something was wrong. *Why did she want to sit by me? Did she get some sort of vibe that I wanted her to? Why would she think that? Did I secretly want her to sit by me and now I have to worry about why I did? I didn't even think anything about her until she got in my face?*

My chest began closing in, my hands started to tingle, and my neck started feeling hot.

Oh no, oh God, this is NOT happening right now. Please no. You have OCD. This is OCD. You have OCD. This is OCD. You have OCD. This is OCD. You have OCD.

It was too late. The panic wouldn't stop and this girl would not shut up and get out of my space. I looked at the guy I had been staring and drooling over just minutes prior. *Didn't that really happen?* I wanted to feel the attraction to him again to prove I really felt it and was not really attracted to women. *Didn't I just feel attracted to a guy? Was I lying? Do I really not find him attractive?* All I could feel was increasing anxiety. *Why did this girl have to come in here? Why did she have to pick me to sit by? What if I saw her and gave her some look subconsciously beckoning her to come over here? If I know I have OCD, why am I feeling panic about this girl in my face and whether or not I want her to be? If I really have OCD, wouldn't I just be able to say it is OCD and not have anxiety? What if I really am attracted to her and that is why I'm having anxiety? What if this OCD diagnosis is all just bullshit and I really am supposed to be gay? What if they just made up this diagnosis to shut me up? I haven't felt these feelings in over a year, why have they returned now? How can I go back to how I was before this stupid girl got into my face?*

"Uh, excuse me, I need to go to the bathroom," I said, bolting out of my seat toward the doors leading out of the Psychology building. I jumped behind the bushes, grabbing the side of the building. Squatting down, I leaned my face against the cold, gritty bricks, and began crying.

Why is this happening? I thought I had a brain disorder! Shouldn't knowing I have OCD make this go away? It's been a full year since I've had these thoughts. Why now? What if I don't really have OCD? What if all this is real? If it wasn't real, wouldn't it just go away when I got my diagnosis?

Several minutes passed before I cooled down and composed my breathing. I wondered if this was a fluke and I just got caught off guard. *Yes, that's it. This is just a stupid test or something to remind me I have OCD and to be more vigilant.* But, the idea of walking into the classroom and seeing that girl again made me panic. *Why am I panicking about some stupid girl I've never met before? I don't even think she is really pretty!* I thought about the guy in the back corner I considered handsome. *How could I have gone from being attracted to this guy one second to worrying I may have to be gay the next? It doesn't make sense! I should know this isn't real if it is OCD. Since I still have these fears, it must mean I really don't have OCD.*

I covered my face with my hands, sobbing. *How did I get here again? What if I really don't have OCD and this is just what my life is? What if the psychologist was lying to cover up I have to be gay? How can I prove that I was really attracted to the guy in the class and not the girl?*

I needed to get back to class. My heart raced as I walked through the front doors of the Psychology building. I couldn't believe not long before, when I entered those same doors, I had no fear at all. My life had entirely changed in mere minutes. I wished I could go back to earlier that day. My breathing quickened as I approached the classroom. *How was I going to sit behind her the entire class wondering if I was attracted to her or not?* Taking a deep breath, I opened the door, and nodded at the professor in apology as I snuck to my seat. I stared at the floor terrified to look at anyone in the classroom. I wanted to look at the guy in the back, but worried I really didn't want to look at him and was lying to myself trying to prove something that wasn't true. Keeping the panic under control took every ounce of energy and concentration.

I slid into my seat, shutting my eyes. I couldn't look at the professor because the girl's blonde hair was in my view. I thought her hair style was cute, so I began questioning whether liking her hair proved I was supposed to date women. Every time she moved, I fearfully braced myself in case she might turn around in my face again. So panicked, I began to worry I couldn't stop thinking about it and panicking must really prove I wanted her secretly because my reaction proved I was attracted to her and not to the guy in the back which meant I had to be gay. It was so irrational it seemed almost comical, yet I couldn't stop engaging in the cycle of fear.

By the time class ended, I was exhausted. I hadn't heard a word the professor said. Before the girl had a chance to turn her head, I grabbed my bag and bolted out the door. I skipped the rest of my classes, went straight home and dove under the covers. I was relieved and safe at home, but couldn't stop thinking what would happen tomorrow. Every time I thought about the class, I started panicking. *Should I drop the class? No, I needed it for graduation. What if she is in my other classes? What if I fail them because I won't be able to pay attention because of her? Does that mean I'd fail because of worry or fail because I'm attracted to her and cannot concentrate?* My world was crumbling. How did this happen so fast? One minute I was a normal person, the next everything about me was in question. I was riddled with anxiety. I couldn't see clearly. I couldn't think about anything but what happened. Even thinking of the Psychology building caused panic. The fear was all-encompassing. It didn't make sense.

It was time for cross-country practice. I knew running would help, so I was eager to go. I met up with the team and we ran an easy six miles. I felt calm and more optimistic after the workout. *Maybe it is just a bad day and this will all go away now.* We headed to the tennis courts where the athletic department put Gatorade outside for the athletes. Everyone was standing around talking and stretching when all of a sudden the guys got really quiet, mumbling under their breath. I looked up to see a female tennis player getting Gatorade. I didn't think much about it because I'd seen her around practice before. But then she walked through the middle of us. All the guys were fawning over her because she was ripped and wore the skimpiest tennis outfit any of us had ever seen. The guys were googly-eyed over her, all the girls were calling her derogatory names, and I was hanging onto the brick wall in a panic worried whether or not I should feel attracted to her because maybe I'm supposed to be gay.

I had seen this girl a hundred times in the last year and had never experienced one ounce of panic or anxiety. In fact, I'd talked to her several times in the weight room before and it wasn't ever a big deal. I always thought she was cool. But now, I couldn't even look at her.

Why did I panic when I saw her? What if I think she is attractive? What if all of a sudden I am attracted to her sexually? Was I attracted to her sexually before? I don't think I was, but what if I am lying to myself and I really am?

I lied to my teammates telling them I had to go work on a project. I went straight to my house, into my room, and under the covers again. I wanted to disappear. I wanted to be anywhere but there. I wanted to be anyone but myself. *What if this isn't OCD? If it is really OCD I would not be having these thoughts because I would know it is only OCD or I would be able to control them because I know it is OCD and it isn't real. Maybe I don't really have OCD, and this is what it is really like? Maybe I have to date women because these anxiety feelings will never go away? But, I know that is not what I want, or what if I am lying to myself? But, if I really don't want to be with women but I can't stop worrying I am supposed to be, does this mean I have to learn to like it because I don't believe I will ever like it and I don't want to have to try to like it? OH MY GOD?! Why has this been okay for so many months and now it is horrible?*

I barely slept. I woke up hoping it would be gone, but the anxiety slapped me in the face when I sat up. I thought about my class and felt overwhelmed with anxiety. I wanted to avoid the Psychology building, but how could I? All my classes were there. *How can I go to cross-country practice and be around the athletic building after yesterday? What if I run into that tennis player? How is it possible I have seen her, talked to her, and never thought anything about it? All of a sudden, the thought of her makes me panicky and scared I may be attracted to her but wasn't before, but maybe I was lying before and now I really was?*

I can't miss class because of this shit. I have to prepare myself before I leave the house. I need to focus.

Focus, Chrissie.

I have OCD. All of these thoughts are from OCD. They are not coming from me. They are coming from my brain with OCD. You can outthink this, Chrissie. You are smarter than this stupid brain disorder.

I left the house feeling confident in my OCD mantra. But, every step closer to the Psychology building broke my confidence. It felt like a balloon was blowing up inside me and it was getting larger the closer I got to the building. I was afraid the balloon would burst and I'd freak out in front of everyone. A low, piercing sound raced past me. I looked up to see the handsome guy from class speed by me on his motorcycle. He turned the corner up ahead and drove back around where I was walking. He parked his bike, looked my direction, and flashed a smile. My heart fluttered and my knees wobbled. I looked around to make sure he was smiling at me and not someone behind me. He waved, confirming I was the one. I couldn't believe he remembered me. And dear God, he looked so hot on that motorcycle in his leather jacket.

Then I remembered how I was supposed to be contemplating whether or not I should turn gay. He had momentarily snatched me out of my stupid anxiety cycle. *This doesn't make sense. How am I completely preoccupied with worrying about something I know I am not, only to get distracted by an attraction I know isn't fake but am going to worry isn't real? This is so ridiculous! How can I be so stupid to engage in this?*

But, did my heart really jump in my chest when he smiled at me? Did I really feel that weak-kneed feeling? Was it real or did I imagine it? What if I faked it to pretend I liked it?

And before I knew it, I was pulled back into the cycle. I questioned everything about the encounter. Even though I knew rationally I was attracted to him, OCD would not let me see it as fact without some sort of 'proof' or 'disproof'. It was maddening.

The irony is I believe there is a monstrous, evil force hijacking the switchboard of my mind. But in reality, there isn't a monster and there isn't any secondary reasoning. The monster is my need and lack of capability to rationalize irrational thoughts and fears. The monster is my own thoughts, putting emphasis on how these thoughts define my existence, and taking pleasure in infiltrating every facet of my life. I don't want this to happen and I rationally know there is no truth behind the fears. But, I can't surrender to my undying need for certainty. And it is exacerbated because I can't accept the difference between who I am as a person and who I am as an OCD sufferer. They have become exhaustingly intertwined.

It is like fighting a boa constrictor in my mind. I wrestle and squirm hoping and praying I may have a slight chance of escaping, but the snake uses my fighting against me to ensnare me. I become so entrenched in the fight I cannot move anymore, I cannot breathe anymore, and I am forced to relent into surrendering to loss of hope and faith; and all the while believing it is something I have caused, something I have done wrong, and something I must deserve. The harder I fight, the worse it becomes. This defining entrapment of OCD has kept me stuck, alone, and saturated in fear almost my entire life. It is a cycle I cannot break by outthinking, outsmarting, or fighting harder; however it tricks me into believing if I just tried a little bit harder, I may be able to win. It doesn't matter how smart or strong I believe I am, OCD has always defeated me, trapping me by my own self-defeating belief I am nothing more than what my monstrous brain decides I should believe.

And there I was again, in the same position as a year ago before I walked down to the creek. I could see no way out. I could see no glimmer of hope. I couldn't see any reason my life would move or evolve past that point. I couldn't see any way to live and manage this horrible disorder. This wasn't living, this felt like dying, all over again.

Chapter 32: Can I Actually Control This?

I felt tortured as the cycle repeated itself every single day and I could do nothing to stop It. My compulsions were driving my thoughts and actions. I avoided getting to class early so the girl would not be able to talk to me. I hated the Psychology building because the thought of it sent me into a freefall of anxiety. I had to walk around the entire campus to avoid it for my other classes. I avoided the hot guy even though he kept trying to talk to me. It was too exhausting trying to prove if I was really attracted to him or if I was faking it to prove I was or was not attracted to him. I left cross-country practice early, avoiding the athletic complex. I even experienced anxiety when drinking Gatorade, worrying that I only wanted to drink it to remember the tennis player. When I saw Gatorade commercials, I quickly turned off the TV to avoid the anxiety.

Triggers were everywhere. My avoidance compulsions caused my world to shrink. When I saw friends, I worried I was only happy to see them because I may be secretly attracted to them. I even worried when I saw friends I didn't necessarily believe were attractive, which I didn't understand. *If I don't actually think they are attractive, why was I worried about being attracted to them?* But, even with the puzzling discrepancies and reminders I actually had a mental illness, the symptoms were too powerful to overcome. I spiraled downward, sinking into suicidal thoughts again.

The following Monday morning, I awoke after another night with barely any sleep, the sixth night in a row I hadn't slept well. I could not concentrate on anything, and every waking moment was consumed with 'what if's' and 'proof and disproof'. I climbed out of bed, started walking toward the bathroom, and collapsed onto the floor. I was too tired to fight anymore. I wanted to die. I was numb and detached because of exhaustion. I saw no reason to live anymore and felt unsafe alone.

I screamed to my roommate, Allison. She came in, lifted me up, and helped me to her room. I lay on the floor sobbing in pain and misery. She was speechless. I had hidden this from her out of embarrassment and shame. She had known something was off, but had no idea it was this bad. She instructed me to call my parents immediately or she was going to do so. She asked if I was still on my medication. I shamefully told her I had stopped taking it months ago. She rightfully scolded me for my decision, instructing me to start taking it again immediately. I did everything she said. I needed someone to tell me what to do because I was so sick and lost. She stayed with me, helping me put myself together to face the day.

I did not realize until she became so angry with me, that all of this was a result of not taking medication. It never crossed my mind that not being on medication could cause things to flare up this way. *Was all this a result of not being medicated? But, the feelings are so real, how can they be attributed to something so simple as not being medicated?* I was astonished at the impact my medication made in managing my symptoms. I was also astonished at how sick with symptoms I could become and how quickly it could happen. I was in desperate need of help with my mental illness. OCD is no joke. The disorder was not something I could control with willpower or strength. I needed professional help. I needed to learn how to live and manage my OCD without the fear of the episodes happening all the time.

After realizing the connection between medication and behavior, I dedicated myself to serious research on OCD. There had to be alternatives to medication, even if supplementary. I was prepared to be on medication my entire life if last week was an indication of how life would be without it. But, I wanted to research other beneficial options too. I needed better answers than just a daily pill.

It took several days of internet searching to find relevant information on the OCD fears I experienced. This was 1998 internet. Finally, I typed in the right combination of words, and scrolled down to an article from a therapist named Dr. Phillipson called 'Thinking the Unthinkable'. I felt butterflies in my stomach as I read the first few teaser lines underneath the title on the search engine page.

> *A man is involved in sexual relations with his female lover. Just prior to orgasm, the thought of his friend Bob pops into his head. This is the fourth time in a month that this has happened. In response to this, he becomes very upset and wonders whether he is gay. He terminates sexual activity in order to avoid having to deal with this concern.*

As I waited for the page to load, my heart beat in my throat. I had only read half the article before I heard myself chanting, "Oh my god....oh my GOD...oh MY GOD....OH MY GOD!" This article described everything I had experienced in my life from age eight until now in impeccable detail. I clicked every tab and highlighted word on Dr. Phillipson's website. I couldn't soak up the information fast enough.

The label for my type of OCD is called 'Pure O', short for 'Purely Obsessional'. While the title didn't make sense semantically, Dr. Phillipson explained in detail how individuals with this type of OCD experience mental obsessions and mental compulsions in different forms. These compulsions include but are not limited to ruminating, avoidance, prayer rituals, and others primarily in the mind. This information summed up my life. I could not believe an entire branch of OCD focused specifically on how my mind worked. This also meant there were other people with my fears. I felt exhilarated!

For the first time, I didn't feel like a crazy freak. I didn't feel like an alien anymore. I imagined so many other people knew exactly what it was like to think like me, react like me, and exist in a mind like mine. I didn't have to feel alone anymore. I was a 'Pure O' sufferer. I was part of a community of people who understood. I was not a lone survivor battling these complex, horrendous, thoughts on my own. I was part of a group. I would be understood and accepted unconditionally for what I had been through. I felt relieved. I felt a worthy and deserving human being.

Dr. Phillipson's research and site indicated there was effective treatment to combat 'Pure O' called Cognitive Behavioral Therapy (CBT) and Exposure Response Prevention (ERP). The graduate stories on the site were true indicators the therapy worked. I was intrigued. I did not care what the therapy cost, how difficult it was, or what I had to do; I just knew I needed to do this CBT/ERP.

I immediately wrote an email to Dr. Phillipson explaining my symptoms and the suicide attempt. I asked if he thought I really had OCD and if I did, would he consider working with me. My hands were shaking as I clicked 'Send'. *What if he reads my email and doesn't think I have OCD? What if he treated all these other people successfully, but the treatment doesn't work on my OCD? What if I go through the treatment and all it does is prove I don't really have OCD?* A cycle of 'what if's' plagued my mind for the next twenty-four hours. But, there was nothing I could do until I heard from him. No matter how agonizing, I had to be patient and wait.

I logged into my email the next day and saw it. The email from Dr. Phillipson was waiting to be opened.

I hesitated. My heart beat so hard and fast my chest was moving. I worried there would only be one sentence reading:

I am so sorry, Chrissie, but you do not really have 'Pure O', you are really just a crazy idiot that will never have a normal life.
  Sincerely, Dr. Phillipson

I had to know for sure, so I braced myself and clicked open the email. I felt immediate relief seeing at least a full paragraph. I read through every line slowly and carefully. A smile began spreading across my face as the closing sentence indicated setting up a consultation for the following week.

If he wants to set up a consultation, he must believe I really have 'Pure O' and I will benefit from ERP. He must believe I will be able manage this and live a normal life, right?

But wait, he never specifically wrote, 'Yes, you have 'Pure O'. What if he wants to do the consultation to find out if I do or if I don't? Why would he waste his time if he really didn't think I did? What if I accidentally lied in the email or exaggerated trying to make him believe I have OCD when I really don't? What if HE lied in the email thinking I really don't have OCD but just wants to make sure?

I reread our email exchange at least twenty times. I carefully deconstructed each sentence making sure it meant and intended what it was supposed to mean and intend. I became caught up in meanings that could be misinterpreted differently by him and by me. I needed to know the one-hundred percent truth. I started to reply to his email to ask for clarification on whether he truly believed I had 'Pure O' or not, but suddenly stopped. *What if he gets irritated with my email and decides not to have a consultation? What if he thinks my email is too forceful and he thinks I'm trying to prove I did or didn't have it? What if he reconsiders having a consultation if I write back to him?*

I began to panic. My chest started closing in and my hands and arms began feeling numb. I needed to close the computer before my anxiety completely took over. *Focus on the upcoming consultation. I can wait to get answers I need and want when I talk to him. Until then, I need to hang onto the hope I have 'Pure O' and there is effective treatment for it.*

I knew it would be a long few days until I could ask him all the questions I needed answering immediately. I had to trust my instinct. I had to trust the process. I had to trust and hope everything would be okay.

Chapter 33: You Want Me To Do WHAT?

The consultation couldn't have arrived sooner. I was eager to hear what Dr. Phillipson had to say. I called his office, announcing to his secretary who I was and our appointment time. She put me on hold. I anticipated what his voice would sound like. I worried he would get on the phone, I wouldn't be able to talk, and I would blow my chances at ERP therapy. I held my breath when heard a click. His deep voice penetrated the silence. I tried responding coolly and collectedly, but I could hear how desperate and erratic my voice sounded.

He asked about my symptoms. I went into great detail concerning my two main obsessions. I experienced a nagging feeling, worrying I was exaggerating. My brain wouldn't stop cycling about being a phony trying to convince this specialist about symptoms I didn't really have. *What the hell is this? I've waited this long to talk to someone who understands, and now I can barely tell the story out of fear I am possibly lying? I know I'm not lying! This shit has happened for YEARS and I am sick of it!* I could barely articulate my thoughts while my brain was so preoccupied with trying to prove the reality of what I was saying. I was so pissed and scared I might blow my chance at therapy.

I described the confusing feelings I had over anxiety about the gay fears. When I finished, he asked a question that made me want to throw the phone across the room. He asked if I ever felt weird sensations in my groin when I had the thoughts. I panicked.

Why is he asking this? Is it some sort of test? If I tell the truth, he may tell me because I have the feelings this proves I don't have OCD and the thoughts are real. But, what if I lie and say I don't have the feelings and he says if I don't have those feelings then I must not have OCD and then I get caught in a lie? What if he thinks I'm a disgusting person because I get those feelings? What if these feelings are normal for people with my type of OCD? Oh God, how do I answer this?

I took a deep breath, telling him the truth about having the horrible 'arousal' movement. I related how I worried the feelings 'proved' the thoughts were real, telling him how distressing the feelings were and how I knew they were different from 'actual' arousal, but couldn't find a way to prove or disprove it.

Without offering reassurance, he let me know people with obsessions like mine did experience this 'groinal syndrome' as well. I wanted to scream from excitement! *So, these feelings aren't my fault either! Other people experience this! This is truly part of OCD! I can't believe it! I'm not a weird, crazy, OCD alien!* I told him how relieved and happy I felt to not be alone with the feelings. He explained more about what the 'groinal syndrome' was and why it accompanied the obsessions. My relief at hearing this was overwhelming. That feeling was by far the worst symptom keeping me trapped with OCD. Just knowing I was not the only person experiencing it relieved a great deal of shame and embarrassment.

After thoroughly discussing my thoughts and symptoms, Dr. Phillipson asked if I was taking medication. I told him I had started meds the previous week. He asked me to stop taking the medication in order to participate in ERP. *What?* I was baffled.

"Um...I relapsed after getting off meds a month ago, which is why I went back on them," I replied quizzically.

He said therapy would be more effective if I participated without medication. I did not have to comply, but greater benefits from therapy would occur if I was medication free. He also urged that I needed to be one-hundred percent dedicated to the therapy and homework every week if I wanted it to be effective. He would know with absolute certainty if I did not do the homework or lied about doing it. If I wasn't committed one-hundred percent, he would not work with me. If I was not dedicated one-hundred percent, it was a waste of his time and mine.

He was so confident in his convictions of this therapy, I could not refuse the requests. His certainty in the process gained my trust in his ability to guide me. The assurance in his ability to teach ERP empowered me and I had no clue yet how it even worked. I decided to do anything he asked, believing this therapy would teach me to manage the obsessions. I was inspired, elated, and terrified.

I committed to the requests regarding medication, homework, and the general process of ERP. Hesitation arose because he never affirmed one hundred percent that I actually had the Pure O branch of OCD. I wanted reassurance so badly, but he informed me immediately he wouldn't reassure me during the process. This was disappointing. I decided to believe it was enough 'proof' I actually had Pure O based on his decision to work with me. He was not interested in wasting his time or mine, so this must mean he believed I could be helped.

Entering therapy, I didn't understand reassurance was detrimental to getting proper treatment for OCD. In fact, I knew nothing about what I would endure with ERP. Blind faith guided me about this therapist, what he was doing, and whether I would learn to manage OCD successfully. I was scared, but intuitively knew this was the answer. Something about his voice, his confidence, and his experience made me believe. Even when my OCD was screaming against the therapy, my ability to trust Dr. Phillipson was my focus, my drive, and my inspiration to continue.

First session, I was asked to create a hierarchy based on things I avoided. We started with smaller anxiety triggers, allowing the obsession and anxiety to be present without me reacting. I was to write down in order of ranking highest to lowest, people and places I avoided because of triggers. We started on the low end of the anxiety scale to learn how therapy worked. Each week we would move up the hierarchy to a more challenging anxiety trigger.

This seemed easy enough, until I got my first assignment.

I was required to sit by the tennis courts every single afternoon for a set amount of time. Because of what happened the week before with the tennis player, I began avoiding that area because of the anxiety. I never saw avoidance as a compulsion. I had always seen it as proof that what I was experiencing in my head was real. Dr. Phillipson viewed avoidance as a mental compulsion. The exposure was to sit in the discomfort I felt at the tennis courts. I was terrified to do this. Just thinking about the tennis courts created all-consuming fear. *How will being present at the tennis courts make things better? What if it proves my anxiety is real and possibly proves I have reason to feel anxious because I feel so strongly that it must mean I'm supposed to be gay? What if I get to the tennis courts and cannot handle the anxiety? What if I freak out?*

Then I remembered Dr. Phillipson saying if I did not do my assignments, he would know and would not work with me anymore. Losing this opportunity terrified me more than the tennis courts, so I committed to doing this assignment. *I'll give it one shot, if it works then great, if it doesn't I can always quit.*

I barely slept the night before my first exposure. My head spun with a whirlwind of questions. *What if I freak out while I'm there? What if I cannot breathe? What if being there proves something? What if, what if, what if?* The questioning wouldn't stop. Rationally, it wasn't a big deal to sit by the stupid tennis courts. I spent three years getting Gatorade in that very spot after practice and never felt anxiety. Now, the building up of knowing I had to be there the next day was overwhelming.

The next morning, I wanted to avoid the assignment altogether. I made excuse after excuse to get out of it. The more time passed, the more anxious I felt about doing it, so I needed to get it over with before I chickened out. Dr. Phillipson would know if I didn't do it, so I committed to the process.

I decided to get it over with before classes. I walked toward the athletic buildings in trepidation. Every step seemed more taxing. My heart beat in my throat. I wanted to turn and sprint in the opposite direction. Rationally, I could not believe how ridiculous I was being, but was too anxious to reason with my thoughts. I wanted to get better and if this was the way to do it. I was determined.

I rounded the corner of the building and saw the spot where we had been standing when the anxiety occurred. A surge of panic shot up my spine. I turned around as my breathing escalated. *It's just OCD, it wants you to feel like this. It wants you to turn around. It doesn't want you to get better. You have to do this. You want to get better. You have to be stronger than OCD. Trust Dr. Phillipson. Trust the process.*

Composing myself, I started down the ramp toward the Gatorade tables. My chest was so tight I thought it might explode. I leaned against the brick wall, slowly sliding to the ground. Taking a deep breath, I pulled out my notebook. The assignment was to sit in the exact spot I felt the anxiety for twenty minutes. I was to rate my anxiety on a scale of 1 (lowest) to 10 (highest) every couple of minutes.

The first rating was a solid 10. My instincts were screaming at me to get the hell out of there. *How in the world is this helping me? What am I doing in this stupid therapy? This isn't going to help? This therapy is putting me in the fire zone! This is making me worse! This is only proving I have good reason to avoid being here!*

I started feeling angry because I was purposely making my levels of anxiety this high. *What am I doing?* I wasn't sure I could stand it anymore. My timer beeped at 2 minutes and I wrote down '10 Plus'. I felt so angry at Dr. Phillipson I was seeing red. I felt angry at the tennis player. I felt angry at my life and my ridiculous brain. I felt angry at normal people. People are so lucky they didn't ever have to worry about things like this. They lived normal lives with no clue how good they had it. My anger was so intense I couldn't believe my timer was already beeping 10 minutes. I tried to gauge my anxiety, but had trouble separating it from my anger. My anger level was a 10 now, but I wasn't sure what to rank my anxiety.

Okay, let's try again. *My anxiety level is a...well, it feels...not high. This cannot be right. I should be more anxious, something must be wrong.* I worried about not being anxious. I scolded myself for not being vigilant enough and that any minute something bad could happen and I wouldn't be able to control it. I concentrated on feeling anxious. The more I tried to increase my anxiety, the harder it was. I argued with my brain to produce anxiety. *Why is my brain not cooperating when I need to he serious about treatment? What if something is wrong? Do I really not have OCD? What if this treatment proves I don't have OCD and I am really crazy and all of my obsessions are real? What if I'm not feeling anxious because I really am okay with the gay thoughts? Am I okay with the thoughts? Does that mean I want to have the thoughts or is that what is supposed to happen with this therapy?* My anxiety surged slightly when thinking these new, bizarre thoughts. So I engaged in them the same way I was supposed to when confronting the tennis courts. *If I use the language Dr. Phillipson recommends, perhaps I can trigger my OCD and have high ratings of anxiety. Here goes:*

If this therapy proves I don't have OCD, I guess I will deal with it when I know for sure. Perhaps I've never had OCD and I've made all this up. Maybe it has all been a cover up since my suicide attempt. Maybe the therapist really did lie to me just to shut me up. Maybe I really am supposed to be gay and he just didn't want to tell me.

I couldn't believe I was allowing myself to utter these sentences. This made me feel legitimately crazy! But as I flooded my mind with these statements and time passed, it became harder to hold onto the '10 plus' anxiety rating. The more I forced feeling anxious, the less the anxiety became. Also, the longer I tried to hold those thoughts in my mind, the more my mind would wonder about other things. I clenched my fists and teeth, concentrating so hard to make the anxiety worse, but it wasn't working. The beeping of my timer cut through my thoughts. I had surpassed 20 minutes at the tennis courts.

The final rating of anxiety in my notebook as I got up to leave was 4. I was confused and hopeful. *Is this what Dr. Phillipson meant when he said being present in the anxiety would make it easier?* I didn't want to get my hopes up, so I chose to believe today was a hoax and tomorrow would prove I could not handle the anxiety.

Each morning of that week, I woke suffocating with anticipatory anxiety before the tennis courts exposure. But each day, my anxiety dropped quicker when I got there and I finished with a lower anxiety rating than the day before. I recognized more exposure to the tennis courts equaled less anxiety. I could hardly believe this was working.

I felt elated but cautious by the end of the week. I could see these exercises might help me knock out the avoidance areas, but I worried maybe this exposure was a fluke. *What if it works for the tennis courts, but it won't work for the others? This still doesn't answer the real question of whether or not the thoughts will ever go away. When will that happen? How will exposing myself to these things answer that question of whether or not I might turn gay one day?*

I couldn't wait to talk to Dr. Phillipson about the result of the assignment. When we spoke on the phone, I felt excited and hopeful. I told him every detail about the tennis courts and I how positive I felt. He seemed pleased, but still wouldn't give me any reassurance about actually having Pure O. He acted very 'business as usual', wanting to move onto next week's assignment. It disappointed me that he didn't seem excited or enthusiastic about the successful exposure.

Before moving to the next assignment, I addressed the issue of the obsession. I asked if the end result of the therapy would finally prove I was not supposed to be gay. His answer shocked me.

He explained the point of therapy wasn't to prove or disprove anything. I wouldn't have any more answers by the end of therapy than I did right then. Answering the question of whether I would be gay one day or not was irrelevant. The point of the therapy was to live with the uncertainty of never knowing for sure whether I was or was not gay. Therapy didn't make the thoughts go away, it made you not react to the thoughts.

WHAT THE HELL? WHAT AM I DOING THIS THERAPY FOR?

I wanted to scream that he was a phony! I wanted to throw my telephone across the room and run screaming into the street. *I don't understand the point of even doing therapy if it won't make these thoughts go away? Why am I putting myself through torture if in the end I won't have answers?*

My anxiety was so high I could barely speak. I started crying. Dr. Phillipson recognized my discomfort and asked me to tell him more. I explained my frustration and misunderstanding of the point of therapy. Talking it through helped calm my anxiety as he listened intently. While he never offered reassurance, he informed me other Pure O sufferers had experienced the same frustration and feelings. It helped me feel less alone to hear him say that. He urged me to trust the process and focus on the homework assignments.

My OCD was screaming to hang up on this guy and forget this stupid therapy, but I was sick of giving power to my OCD. I was tired of fighting the same cycle and battle every day. It was time to try something different. It was time to take the risk and see if it worked. If it didn't work, I'd figure out something else. *I'm here now and I'm going to commit to the therapy even though I don't fully understand it or believe it can actually work.*

I calmed down, letting him know I was committed to the therapy and would try to trust the process.

And then he told me what my next assignment was to be.

"YOU WANT ME TO...WHAT???" I exclaimed.

"I have to sit on a bench I have been avoiding because I felt anxious there when a girl sat down beside me and started chatting with me out of the blue and I worried it was because she thought I was giving her some vibe I didn't know about and she probably thought I was attracted to her when I really wasn't? I have to spend a half-hour sitting on the bench I hate every day and rate women walking by on a scale of 1-10 on their attractiveness! WHAT? NO! WHAT? NO!"

"You don't want to do the homework?" Dr. Phillipson asked.

"Yes. No, I don't want to. Okay I'll try, but what if I can't do it? No, I can't do it. Oh my God, there's no way? Oh God. Okay, yes sir, I will do it. But, I am scared! What if I rate people as attractive and find I really don't have OCD? Can't you just tell me I really do have OCD? Why won't you confirm this is really OCD? I'd feel better about doing these crazy exposures if I knew you thought I really have it."

"Whether I tell you yes or no isn't going to make a difference. Are you committed to the therapy? If so, you have to learn to take the risk and live with the uncertainty of not knowing all of the answers you want reassurance for," he answered.

Dammit. This is bullshit. I hate this.

"Yes. I am committed. I will do the exposure, I promise."

I hung up, put my pillow over my head, and sobbed uncontrollably. I didn't know what felt worse, the anxiety from OCD or the anxiety about exposures. I felt defeated after that day. *The tennis courts must have been a fluke. All the positivity I had about last week is gone. This next assignment is going to prove I am just crazy and don't have OCD. This is finally going to prove what I've been scared of my whole life. I cannot believe I agreed to this.*

I cried myself to sleep from exhaustion and fear. Tomorrow could be the day I have avoided my whole life; the day proving I really am crazy and stupid, and OCD has been an excuse.

This could be the end of any shred of hope.

Chapter 34: Taking the Risk and Living with Uncertainty

I woke up in a state of panic. I wanted to go back to the tennis courts where everything seemed easier. *How was I going to do this homework? What if I like rating girls? What if I like looking at them? What if the exercise 'proves' I don't have OCD and I am supposed to be gay? What kind of sick doctor wants me to do this? What if he is just screwing with me?*

I slid off my bed, hitting the ground on all fours to manage the panic attack. *Breathe, Chrissie. Remember the tennis courts? You were terrified the first day. Trust the process. Trust the doctor. It's going to feel worse before it gets better.* I took a deep breath and grabbed my notebook. I couldn't believe I was about to do this.

Turning my car onto the street where I could see the bench caused overwhelming anxiety. I avoided this entire area of campus for over a month because of that stupid bench. I slowly got out of the car with my head down and eyes on the ground. Holding back tears, I began walking toward the bench.

I cannot believe I have a disorder where therapy requires me to do such preposterous things to 'get better'? This feels worse than the actual disorder. What if people know what I was out here to do? What if they notice I am looking at them? What if people think I am attracted to them? How will I explain 'this is my homework for my brain disorder to prove I have OCD and I'm not supposed to be gay?' WHAT?! I cannot do this. Why am I putting myself in this position? I hate my doctor. I hate my life. I hate this damn disorder!

I thought about the tennis courts and how hard it was approaching them the first day. But, this seemed different. My anxiety was so high I felt out of control physically. I wanted to run as fast as I could away from there, but I was almost to the bench. I decided since I was already there, I would at least try it one day and decide afterward whether to continue this stupid therapy.

I wanted to sit, calm down, and be present in the anxiety before I started the rating process. I sat down, closing my eyes. *Just let the anxiety be there. Let it take me over. Let's just freak out and get it over with.* But, the more I pressed for a panic attack, the farther away the anxiety seemed. This made me very nervous. *Why am I not panicking anymore? Does this mean I want to rate girls? Does this mean I actually want to be here and do this stupid exercise?* These thoughts spiked my anxiety to a 10. I felt more comfortable being anxious about the assignment than not. This didn't make sense to me, but I was too panicky to process it.

It was now or never to start this assignment. I thought that exercise would be the tell-all whether or not I had OCD, that there would be some kind of proof in this one way or another. So I surrendered to the idea of taking the risk and living with the uncertainty despite the consequences. If it proved something, I would deal with it later. At that moment I just needed to suck it up and try.

The timer on my watch was set for a half-hour, and I wrote a 10 in large letters as my first anxiety rating. I looked up and saw several people walking down the pathway toward the bench. My anxiety was screaming at me to get up and run away. *No! I am going to do this!* I saw a girl in the group. This was it. My heart was pounding with fear. As she got closer, I quickly looked her up and down to rate her attractiveness but she was too far away. My head was pounding with worries about what it 'meant' if I rated her with a high number. No amount of ruminating could get me out of that immediate situation. She was getting closer and I didn't want to stare at her. Once she was a stone's throw away, I appraised her. I thought she was pretty but not '10' pretty, so I gave a rating of '8' on my paper. I rated my anxiety as 20 out of 10. The group walked past me and I could barely hold my composure. *That was miserable. Why am I doing this? This is not helping me, it is making things worse!*

Before I could engage in further worry about doing the exercise, I saw someone walking down the path toward the bench. *Oh crap, it is a girl.* As she approached, my anxiety spiked and I felt I was suffocating. At 8 feet away, I decided to rate her as a '6'. I rated my anxiety as 20 out of 10 again. I looked at her again and felt guilty thinking she was only a '6'. I worried she would think I was an asshole if she knew I rated her lower than the first girl. I chuckled nervously, causing concern I wasn't being serious enough about my anxiety.

I composed myself, knowing I needed to be serious and vigilant. I started wondering what other people would rate me if they were doing that exercise. Was I a 10? Was I an 8? I scolded myself silently for deviating from my anxiety. I needed to focus on being anxious. As other girls approached, I suddenly had a surge of worry that I wanted to rate the girls in comparison to myself. Why wasn't I taking this seriously? I wanted to focus on my anxiety and how horrible this was, but found I couldn't hold the high rates of anxiety.

Five girls were approaching. I was more worried about not having time to assess a fair rating before they walked past me. I didn't want to rate anyone too low because that didn't seem fair. *Focus, Chrissie. Focus on your anxiety and feelings, not on theirs!* I was pissed at myself. Was I not taking this seriously? Why couldn't I feel anxious like I did when I first got there?

When the timer beeped after a half-hour, I was surprised. I had rated every girl walking past me along with my anxiety level rating. My level was always higher if I thought someone had a higher rating. But, I noticed as more time passed, my anxiety lessened when I saw someone approaching and I was seriously inquiring about their rating. I felt guilty when I gave someone a 'lower' rating because I didn't want to seem shallow. I was dumbfounded at the rational contradiction of my thought process. Before the timer went off, I laughed at the reasons why I rated someone high or low. I couldn't believe I was more preoccupied with whether or not I was shallow, than whether or not I worried if I was attracted to them or not. It baffled me that I couldn't hold onto high anxiety in the face of this exposure. I was skeptical whether that day was a fluke and the next would actually prove I didn't have OCD. I guessed I would have to wait and see.

I left the bench with an anxiety level of 4.

Every day the homework assignment became easier. My highest level of anxiety was always in anticipation of the exposure. Once I actually got to the bench and started the rating process, I could barely hold onto an anxiety rating above 5. Each day, I would leave feeling safer and stronger in my diagnosis and the treatment. I was in awe of how this simple act of allowing the anxiety to just be there could have so much power over OCD. I was hopeful. Perhaps I could really live with this disorder and manage it successfully?

In only two weeks of assignments, I felt confident enough to face and conquer the anxiety that had controlled my actions and responses almost my entire life. It was the anxiety I feared, not the obsessions. It was the anxiety that was real, not the obsessions. Once I faced the actual 'trigger' head on, I found no substance for the fear whatsoever. It was the anxiety and thought of the anxiety that was crippling and paralyzing, not the obsessions. It felt liberating.

Dr. Phillipson and I challenged every mental ritual, rumination, and avoidance compulsion with ERP therapy. As I worked through each exposure, my confidence in 'trusting the process' gained momentum. We moved up the hierarchy, and triggers which once seemed terrifying and impossible were now part of the next step to conquering OCD. Each exposure was terrifying at first, but I remembered and used the success from previous exposures as motivation and guide to help me move through the fear. My mantra was 'take the risk and live with the uncertainty'. The success of my recovery was entirely contingent on the extent of my commitment to treatment.

It took a couple months to move through my hierarchy of exposures. By the time we reached the top, I already knew the treatment was a success. I knew, because I understood and respected the process. The key to conquering this disorder was absolute awareness and undeniable faith in my ability to execute a process which seemed unnatural to everything I'd ever known prior. To have power over OCD, I needed to go against every instinct OCD had fooled me into believing. From now on I would toe the line of uncertainty while challenging what I believed to be my innate sense of self and knowledge. I had to recognize everything driving my actions and reactions the past twelve years had been the trickery of OCD. I was rewiring my brain how to think.

It hardly made sense, but I had no other choice than to throw caution to the wind and take a chance on a therapy harder than the actual disorder. Every week it seemed easier to deny the assignments and give in to the compulsions, to temporarily ease my anxiety. And I was tempted every week! But, something inside knew therapy was the key to living successfully with my disorder no matter how farfetched the assignments seemed. I found hope in the countless patients Dr. Phillipson had treated successfully before me. I battled every doubt telling me I was the exception and couldn't get better. I wrestled with the worry I was the one person he could not treat successfully. I worried every day the therapy would only result in me finding out I really didn't have OCD and the thoughts were real. I ignored every lying OCD instinct telling me I could never live without the constant worry. I somehow found strength and hope to trust my doctor and trust the process when hope seemed too far to reach.

The day came when Dr. Phillipson informed me I no longer needed him. I completed the final exposure and had graduated from ERP. I was elated and terrified. It had worked! I had no anxiety or fear surrounding the gay obsession. I never thought it was possible, but it happened. This fear had guided my every thought and action for six years, and now it was no longer relevant. It was a triumph.

It was also scary realizing the battle I had fought for so many years was over. *What would I do with myself now? Why did this happen to me? Who am I? What will I do if it comes back? Will it come back? What do I believe now? How can I process the grief of losing twelve years of my life to this disorder?*

These questions and others plagued me the following thirteen years of my life. OCD not only influenced my mindset and worldview, it infiltrated my emotional outlook and perception of my existence and reality in the world. After surviving a suicide attempt, diagnosis, and successful treatment, I entered a phase of my illness almost as detrimental and devastating as the disorder itself; I battled personal stigma while working through the stages of recovery with mental illness. I will address the details, trials, and triumphs of my journey through personal stigma in the sequel to this memoir.

Chapter 35: The Lessons of OCD

Having the courage and determination to take the risk, live with the uncertainty, and partake in Exposure Response Prevention with Dr. Phillipson was the greatest decision and commitment of my life. The therapy did not eliminate the thoughts Pure O produces, but taught me the skills and knowledge to manage the anxiety and face obsessions as they arise. Beginning ERP, I was devastated to learn the therapy wouldn't make the obsessions go away. The thought of believing I could have obsessive thoughts but not react to them was foreign to me. But, my doctor was correct in telling me to trust the process and trust him. By the time I graduated from ERP, I had accomplished many things the world would deem successful for an individual, but I considered conquering the debilitation of OCD as the greatest feat of my life.

As I complete this memoir, it has been thirty years since the onset of OCD and eighteen years since my suicide attempt, hospitalization, and diagnosis. The road I have traveled with the disorder and the internal stigma of mental illness has been extraordinarily difficult. Sometimes I feel the disorder stole part of my life, but at other times I feel incredibly lucky to have had the opportunity to challenge my worldview at such a young age.

Having every tenet challenged and disproved after dedicating my life and existence to them was no easy feat, but I didn't get to choose how my obsessions and compulsions manifested. OCD infiltrated my life through religious beliefs because it was a vulnerable place for me to question and push my boundaries. OCD strikes the places in life you would never expect to be tested. It creates uncertainty in places you never believe doubt can find you. Considering the tormenting and tortuous years I lived without explanation of my symptoms, I take tremendous pride in my strength to live and fight every day, holding onto invisible hope.

The greatest gift my experience with OCD provided is empathetic appreciation for the experiences we endure as human beings. Humanity was the facet which breathed life into me after I truly believed life wasn't worth living.

My experience at the psychiatric facility changed my life and worldview. It eliminated boundaries, broke down walls, and abolished judgment. My faith in the power of empathy, compassion, and the simplicity of humanity was restored. I learned none of us ever truly know what another person is suffering with or through. I learned the importance of resisting judgment. I learned to never underestimate the power of being present for one another with an open mind and open heart. I learned there are people who will take a chance on you even when you believe you aren't worthy of love and acceptance.

Although I tucked these lessons away for many years afterward, I was forever changed by the kindness of the individuals I spent Christmas with behind plated glass and padlocked doors. They never gave up on me, even when I refused to acknowledge the severity and actuality of my mental state. They taught me how much of an impact the smallest gesture can make on someone else's life. They believed in me when I could not find the strength to believe in myself. They saw something inside of me worth believing in, worth accepting, and worth loving. They were my first peer mentors. They were the people who knew me for everything good and bad, and accepted me anyway.

My hope for this memoir is to share my story as a means of helping others feel less alone in their OCD and mental illness. The journey to recovery can be difficult, lonely, and scary, but my hope is you will never give up. Recovery is possible for everyone. You are not an exception to the rule. You are just as capable of recovery as anyone else. Never forget that you are not alone. You are worth recovery. You deserve recovery.

OCD can be overcome. OCD can be managed. You can live a successful life with OCD. It is possible for anyone.

About the Author

Chrissie Hodges is a mental health advocate and public speaker for Obsessive-Compulsive Disorder, mental illness, and stigma reduction. Chrissie works as a certified Peer Support Specialist in private practice and as an Exposure Response Prevention Therapy coach for Effective OCD Treatment. Chrissie sits on the Colorado Advisory Board on Mental Health Standards and Regulations. She co-hosts the podcast on stigma reduction, 'Two Flew Over the Cuckoo's Nest'. She is a Crisis Intervention Team presenter on lived experience with OCD for the Denver Police and Sheriff Departments. Chrissie blogs at 'Battling the OCD Demon' on wordpress.com and is a professional blog and video contributor for 'Mental Health on The Mighty'.

To find out more about Chrissie's advocacy and work, please visit her website at www.chrissiehodges.com or contact her via email at ocd.chrissie@gmail.com.

Printed in the USA
CPSIA information can be obtained
at www.ICGtesting.com
LVHW041048211024
794396LV00007B/90